3

The Researched Essay

EFFECTIVE
Academic Writing

SECOND EDITION

Rhonda Liss
Jason Davis

OXFORD
UNIVERSITY PRESS

OXFORD
UNIVERSITY PRESS

198 Madison Avenue
New York, NY 10016 USA

Great Clarendon Street, Oxford, OX2 6DP, United Kingdom

Oxford University Press is a department of the University of Oxford.
It furthers the University's objective of excellence in research, scholarship,
and education by publishing worldwide. Oxford is a registered trade
mark of Oxford University Press in the UK and in certain other countries

General Manager, American ELT: Laura Pearson
Publisher: Stephanie Karras
Associate Publishing Manager: Sharon Sargent
Managing Editor: Jennifer Meldrum
Director, ADP: Susan Sanguily
Executive Design Manager: Maj-Britt Hagsted
Associate Design Manager: Michael Steinhofer
Image Manager: Trisha Masterson
Electronic Production Manager: Julie Armstrong
Production Artist: Elissa Santos
Production Coordinator: Chris Espejo
Production Coordinator: Brad Tucker

ISBN: 978 0 19 432348 2 EFFECTIVE ACADEMIC WRITING 3 WITH ONLINE
PRACTICE PACK
ISBN: 978 0 19 432343 7 EFFECTIVE ACADEMIC WRITING 3 STUDENT BOOK AS
PACK COMPONENT
ISBN: 978 0 19 433391 7 EFFECTIVE ACADEMIC WRITING ONLINE

Printed in China

This book is printed on paper from certified and well-managed sources

ACKNOWLEDGEMENTS

*The authors and publisher are grateful to those who have given permission to reproduce
the following extracts and adaptations of copyright material:*

p. 38 From "At Some Medical Schools, Humanities Join the Curriculum" by
Randy Kennedy. From *The New York Times*, April 17, 2006 © 2006 The New
York Times. All rights reserved. Used by permission and protected by the
Copyright Laws of the United States. The printing, copying, redistribution,
or retransmission of this Content without express written permission is
prohibited.; p. 73 From "What Makes People Happy? Young Filmmaker Finds
the Answer" by Patricia Xavier, March 11, 2004, http://www.youngmoney.
com. Reprinted by permission of Young Money, LLC. (Not a part of Incharge
Education Foundation); p. 107 From "Japanese Man Found Guilty of Online
Move Theft" Agence France Press, December 2004. AGence France-Press
International News (Online Citations), Copyright 2004 by Agence France-
Presse (U.S.) Reproduced with permission of Agence France-Presse (U.S.)
in the format Textbook via Copyright Clearance Center; p. 114 From
"Plagiarism Lines Blur for Students in Digital Age" by Trip Gabriel. From
The New York Times, August 2, 2010, © 2010 The New York Times. All rights
reserved. Used by permission and protected by the Copyright Laws of the
United States. The printing, copying, redistribution, or retransmission of this
Content without express written permission is prohibited; p. 116 Adapted
from "Historian Who Chronicled The Roosevelts Admits Plagiarism" by

Rupert Cornwell, *The Independent* March 3, 2002: Foreign News 14. Reprinted
by permission of The Independent; p. 134 From "Why Cell Phones and
Driving Don't Mix" by Lee Dye, June 29, 2005 as appeared on http://abcnews.
go.com. Reprinted by permission of ABC News Program; p. 143 Adapted
from "Learn Soft Skills to Gain a Tougher Edge in the Job Market" by Steve
McCormack, *The Independent,* March 30, 2011, p. 2. Reprinted by permission
of The Independen.; p. 179 From "The Shepherd's Daughter" from *The Daring
Young Man on the Flying Trapeze* by William Saroyan. used with permission
of Trustees of Leland Stanford Junior University; p. 206 From *The Images
of Chekov,* translated by Robert Payne, translation copyright © 1963 and
copyright renewed 1991 by Alfred A. Knopf, Inc. used by permission of
Alfred A. Knopf, a division of Random House, Inc.

Illustrations by: p. 71 Supertotto; p. 72 Supertotto; p. 105 Jonathan Keegan;
p. 106 Jonathan Keegan.

*We would also like to thank the following for permission to reproduce the following
photographs:*

Cover, Design Pics/The Irish Image Collection/Getty Images; viii, Marcin
Krygier/iStockphoto (laptop); p. vi, Opener, Writing Process and Review
pages, 203 stocksnapper/ istockphoto (letter texture); p. 1 Eliane SULLE/
Alamy; p. 2 Eliane SULLE/Alamy (student male); p. 2 Fancy/Alamy (man);
p. 2 PhotosIndia.com LLC/Alamy (girl); p. 35 Oliver Rossi/Corbis UK Ltd.;
p. 36 Oliver Rossi/Corbis UK Ltd. (kite); p. 36 Jose Luis Pelaez, Inc./Blend /
Corbis UK Ltd. (father); p. 48 Margaret Bourke-White/Time Life Pictures/Getty
Images (school); p. 48 Alfred Eisenstaedt/Time & Life Pictures/Getty Images
(children); pp. 67, 102, 138, 175, 206 Monkey Business Images/Shutterstock
(Clock); p. 67 Ricki Rosen Saba/Corbis UK Ltd. (skipping); p. 67 Kim Kyung-
Hoon/Reuters/Corbis UK Ltd. (football); p. 177 TIME & LIFE Images/Richard
Howard/Getty Images; p. 178 TIME & LIFE Images/Richard Howard/Getty
Images (Wheelchair); p. 178 Hulton Archive/Nancy R. Schiff/Getty Images
(Pritchett).

Reviewers

We would like to acknowledge the following individuals for their input during the development of the series:

Chris Alexis, College of Applied Sciences, Sur, Oman

Amina Saif Mohammed Al Hashamia, College of Applied Sciences, Nizwa, Oman

Amal Al Muqarshi, College of Applied Sciences, Ibri, Oman

Saleh Khalfan Issa Al-Rahbi, College of Applied Sciences, Nizwa, Oman

Dr. Debra Baldwin, UPP, Alfaisal University, Saudi Arabia

Virginia L. Bouchard, George Mason University, English Language Institute, Washington D.C.

Judith Buckman, College of Applied Sciences, Salalah, Oman

Dr. Catherine Buon, American University of Armenia, Armenia

Mei-Rong Alice Chen, National Taiwan University of Science and Technology, Taipei

Mark L. Cummings, Jefferson Community and Technical College, KY

Hitoshi Eguchi, Hokusei Gakuen University, Japan

Elizabeth W. Foss, Washtenaw Community College, MI

Sally C. Gearhart, Santa Rosa Junior College, CA

Alyona Gorokhova, Miramar Community College, CA

Dr. Simon Green, College of Applied Sciences, Oman

Janis Hearn, Hongik University, South Korea

Adam Henricksen, University of Maryland, Baltimore County, MD

Clay Hindman, Sierra College, CA

Kuei-ping Vicky Hsu, National Tsing Hua University, Hsinchu

Azade Johnson, Abu Dhabi Men's College, Higher Colleges of Technology, U.A.E.

Chandra Johnson, Fresno Pacific University, CA

Pei-Lun Kao, Chang Gung University, Gueishan

Yuko Kobayashi, Tokyo University of Science, Japan

Blair Lee, Kyung Hee University, Japan

Chia-yu Lin, National Tsing Hua University, Hsinchu

Kent McClintock, Chosun University, South Korea

Joan Oakley, College of the North Atlantic-Qatar, Qatar

Fernanda G. Ortiz, CESL University of Arizona, AZ

William D. Phelps, Southern Illinois University, IL

Dorothy Ramsay, College of Applied Sciences, Sohar, Oman

Vidya Rangachari, Mission College, CA

Elizabeth Rasmussen, Northern Virginia Community College, VA

Syl Rice, Abu Dhabi Men's College, Higher Colleges of Technology, U.A.E.

Donna Schaeffer, University of Washington, WA

Dr. Catherine Schaff-Stump, Kirkwood Community College, IA

Mary-Jane Scott, Sungshin Women's University, South Korea

Jenay Seymour, Hong-ik University, South Korea

Janet Sloan Rachidi, U.A.E. University, Al Ain, U.A.E.

Bob Studholme, U.A.E. University, Al Ain, U.A.E.

Paula Suzuki, SI-UK Language Centre, Japan

Sabine Thépaut, Intensive English Language Institute, University of North Texas, TX

Shu-Hui Yu, Ling Tung University, Taichung

Author Acknowledgments

We would first like to thank our tireless editor Vicky Aeschbacher for her insights, expertise, and lively input. We could always depend on her for immediate feedback and a wealth of creative suggestions. We also thank Sharon Sargent, Stephanie Karras, and Michael Incardona for their positive energy, enthusiasm, and support.

We are grateful to our students in the CUNY Language Immersion Program whose struggles with the English language were the inspiration and backbone for the activities in this book. Their amazing and invigorating stories enhanced our own journey.

Thank you, Dr. Reid Strieby for your constructive criticism and enduring support. Finally, we would like to thank each other for always keeping our goal in sight, our energy alive, and our humor intact.

R.L and J.D.

Contents

Unit	Academic Focus	Critical Thinking and Research Focus	Rhetorical Focus	Language and Grammar Focus
5 Classification Essays page 141	Career Planning	**Critical Thinking Focus** • Reading and analyzing bar graphs **Research Focus** • Paraphrasing a bar graph	• Classification organization • Establishing order of importance, degree, and size	• Gerunds and infinitives • Verbs following *make*, *let*, and *have*
6 Reaction Essays page 177	Literary Analysis	**Critical Thinking Focus** • Theme in short stories **Research Focus** • Works cited list	• Reaction organization • The literary present	• Passives

APPENDICES

Welcome to Effective Academic Writing

Effective Academic Writing, Second Edition instills student confidence and provides the tools necessary for successful academic writing.

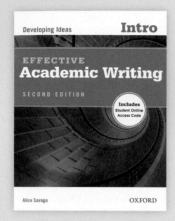

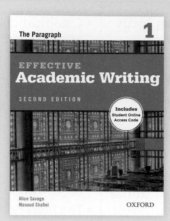

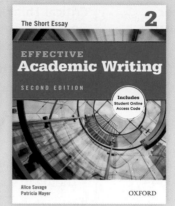

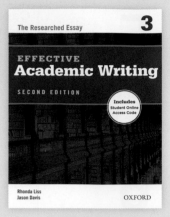

Introductory Level
Developing Ideas

Level 1
The Paragraph

Level 2
The Short Essay

Level 3
The Researched Essay

- Step-by-step **Writing Process** guides and refines writing skills.

- **Timed writing** practice prepares students for success on high-stakes tests.

- **Online Writing Tutor** improves academic writing inside and outside the classroom.

GO ONLINE

Online Writing Support for all Levels

Overview

Effective Academic Writing, Second Edition delivers practice that will improve your students' writing.

- NEW! The new **Introductory Level** provides students with the support and instruction they need for writing success in the lowest-level writing courses.
- NEW! **More content-area related assignments** with more academic vocabulary and readings prepare students for the challenges of the academic classroom.

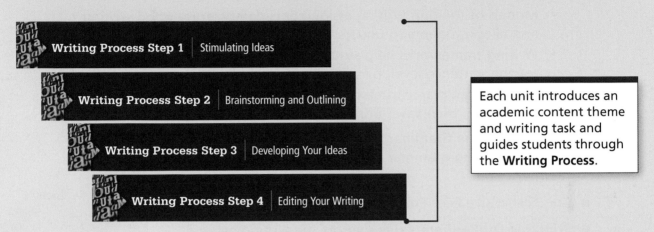

Writing Process Step 1	Stimulating Ideas
Writing Process Step 2	Brainstorming and Outlining
Writing Process Step 3	Developing Your Ideas
Writing Process Step 4	Editing Your Writing

Each unit introduces an academic content theme and writing task and guides students through the **Writing Process**.

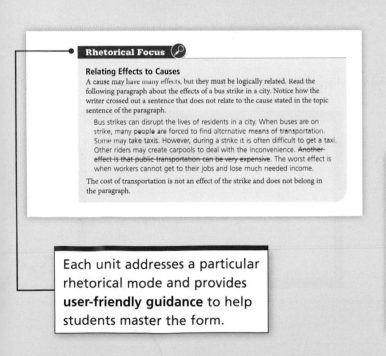

Rhetorical Focus

Relating Effects to Causes
A cause may have many effects, but they must be logically related. Read the following paragraph about the effects of a bus strike in a city. Notice how the writer crossed out a sentence that does not relate to the cause stated in the topic sentence of the paragraph.

Bus strikes can disrupt the lives of residents in a city. When buses are on strike, many people are forced to find alternative means of transportation. Some may take taxis. However, during a strike it is often difficult to get a taxi. Other riders may create carpools to deal with the inconvenience. ~~Another effect is that public transportation can be very expensive.~~ The worst effect is when workers cannot get to their jobs and lose much needed income.

The cost of transportation is not an effect of the strike and does not belong in the paragraph.

Each unit addresses a particular rhetorical mode and provides **user-friendly guidance** to help students master the form.

Concise and effective language and grammar presentations develop students' understanding and improve their accuracy.

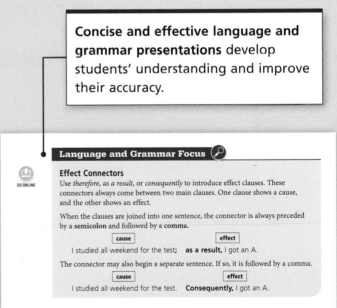

Language and Grammar Focus

GO ONLINE

Effect Connectors
Use *therefore*, *as a result*, or *consequently* to introduce effect clauses. These connectors always come between two main clauses. One clause shows a cause, and the other shows an effect.

When the clauses are joined into one sentence, the connector is always preceded by a **semicolon** and followed by a **comma**.

cause	effect

I studied all weekend for the test; **as a result,** I got an A.

The connector may also begin a separate sentence. If so, it is followed by a comma.

cause	effect

I studied all weekend for the test. **Consequently,** I got an A.

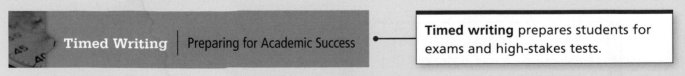

Timed Writing | Preparing for Academic Success

Timed writing prepares students for exams and high-stakes tests.

Effective Academic Writing Online

GO ONLINE **IT'S EASY!** Use the access code printed on the inside back cover of this book to register at www.effectiveacademicwriting.com.

For the Student

- *Online Writing Tutor* helps students retain and apply their writing skills.
  - Models of the unit writing assignments **demonstrate good writing** and allow students to understand how each text is constructed.
  - **Writing frameworks help students with organizing and structuring,** for the sentence level, paragraph level, and the text as a whole.
  - Students can plan, structure, and write their own texts, check their work, **then save, print, or send directly to their teacher.**
- Extensive **Online Grammar Practice** and **grammar term glossary** support students in using grammar structures appropriately and fluently in their writing.
- Comprehensive **Peer Editor's Checklists** support collaborative learning.
- **Printable Outline Templates** support the writing process.

For the Teacher

- **IELTS-style, TOEFL-style, and TOEIC-style online writing tests** can be **customized** and **printed.**
- **Online test rubrics** make grading easy.
- **Online Grammar Practice** is automatically graded and entered into the online grade book.
- Answer keys make grading easy.
- The **online management system** allows you to manage your classes. View, print, or export all class and student reports.

FOR ADDITIONAL SUPPORT
Email our customer support team at eltsupport@oup.com.

FOR TEACHER CODES
Please contact your sales representative for a **Teacher Access Code.** Teacher Access Codes are sold separately.

UNIT 1

The Researched Essay

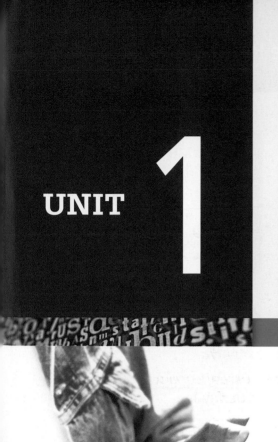

Unit Goals

Critical Thinking Focus

- understanding assignments
- words used to signal rhetorical modes

Research Focus

- collecting information from primary and secondary sources
- guidelines for researching a topic

Rhetorical Focus

- structure of the researched essay
- selecting and narrowing a topic
- unity and coherence

Language and Grammar Focus

- main and dependent clauses
- run-on sentences
- sentence fragments
- verb tense consistency

Exercise 1 Thinking about the topic

Discuss the pictures with a partner.

- What types of writing are the people in the pictures practicing?
- What types of writing do you do in your leisure time?
- What types of writing do people do in professional settings?
- What are some of the challenges you face when you write?

Rhetorical Focus

The Researched Essay

You may have written short essays, but as you progress in your academic studies, your teachers will expect longer essays that have been well researched. These essays have greater **elaboration,** which may include examples, statistics, questions, definitions, quotations, and anecdotes. Researched essays are more analytical in nature.

Like other essays, the researched essay has three basic parts: an **introduction,** a **body,** and a **conclusion.** Each body paragraph contains a **topic sentence** that supports the **thesis statement.** Facts found in research, quotations from experts, and statistics all support the body paragraphs to strengthen the essay's message.

A. Read the essay below about becoming an academic writer. Notice how the essay is organized.

Becoming an Academic Writer

Learning how to write an academic essay is essential for students `introduction` who are planning to attend college. Most professors require critiques of books and films, research papers, and formal reports related to the content of their courses. When I first started college, I was excited about facing these challenges and pursuing my major, media and communications. I was determined to improve my writing. To achieve this goal, I focused on three points: the content of my essays, correct grammar, and advanced-level vocabulary.

As soon as I started to write for college, I discovered that the content of `body paragraph 1` the writing required for my college courses was different from the content I had used in high school. In the past, most of my writing dealt with my personal experiences. I wrote mainly about my family, childhood, and friends. In contrast, college writing focused on a variety of issues that I was unfamiliar with, such as reacting to a piece of literature or writing about science or politics. Therefore, the most important thing for me was to understand the assignment and research the topic before attempting my first draft. I started by reading encyclopedia articles to build a foundation. I researched the topic so that I could include examples, statistics, and direct quotations whenever possible to support my ideas. By giving specific examples, I made my ideas more detailed, easier to read, and much more impressive. However, grammatical problems in my writing were still an issue.

I realized that I had to improve my understanding of grammar `body paragraph 2` to write for college. Before I came to college, grammar was not my strong point. I often created run-on sentences or sentence fragments. In several instances my professors would not accept my writing. Instead, they required that I revise my work before I turned it in for a grade. Consequently, I made grammar my second priority. I reviewed the basic grammatical structures such as subjects and verbs, and I checked all my work for verb-tense consistency and correct punctuation. Soon my sentences became more complex because I included transitions, gerunds, and embedded clauses. The more I wrote, the more my writing improved, and as my grammar improved, my ideas became more convincing since they appeared to be from a more educated person.

Because I was accustomed to writing informally, I usually wrote the way I spoke. It was quite common for me to include slang and abbreviated terms, which were appropriate in social contexts but were not acceptable in formal essays. I soon realized that much of my academic writing required sophisticated vocabulary. Not surprisingly, improving my vocabulary became my third and final goal. I bought a new dictionary and thesaurus to help expand my word knowledge. I became more aware of how often I repeated the same words and phrases throughout my essay. I often searched for synonyms to replace words that I thought were too simple for a college essay. I also focused more on the rules of spelling, and I corrected any errors I found before submitting my assignment to the instructor.

body paragraph 3

Academic writing requires critical thinking skills, an understanding of the topic, research, high-level vocabulary, and correct grammar. Having these skills is empowering since it has made me a better communicator and student. I have come a long way since I started college, and I am now proud of the writing that I produce.

conclusion

B. Answer the questions and respond to the statements below.

1. Underline the thesis statement in the introduction. What three points does the writer suggest that he or she will make in the essay? _____

   _____

2. How does body paragraph 1 relate to the thesis statement? _____

   _____

   _____

3. How does body paragraph 2 relate to the thesis statement? _____

   _____

   _____

4. How does body paragraph 3 relate to the thesis statement? _____

_____

_____

5. What does the conclusion tell readers about the importance of this topic to the writer? _____

_____

Rhetorical Focus

The Introduction

An academic essay's introduction must have a **hook, background information,** and a **thesis statement.**

Hook

A hook is a statement that begins the introduction. It includes one or two interesting sentences that engage the readers' attention and stimulate their curiosity. The sentences below provide the hook for an essay about an economic crisis.

> Henry Paulson's expression turned to horror as he looked down at the numbers. He suddenly realized that the market was on the verge of collapse.

Background Information

The background information contains a general statement or statements that give a broad picture of the subject matter to be discussed. They provide extra information to help the reader understand the content of the essay. The sentences below provide the context (situation) for an essay on the economic crisis of 2008.

> In September 2008 the banking system in the United States nearly collapsed, leading to what many considered to be the worst economic crisis since the Great Depression of the 1930s.

Thesis Statement

A thesis statement usually comes at the end of the introduction. It summarizes what the entire essay is about. It contains the **topic** and the **controlling idea** for the whole essay. The topic is the subject matter of the essay. The controlling idea defines the purpose of the essay and sets its direction.

topic	controlling idea

The economic crisis could have been avoided with banking regulations.

Read this introduction to an essay. Then answer the following questions.

The Risks of Social Media

① Today there are more social networking accounts than there are people on the planet. Social networking allows people to share ideas ② with friends and family everywhere. It connects people in ways that were never possible in the past. Still, users of these sites should be cautious. Social media can be dangerous. ③

1. Circle and label the hook. How does it engage readers? _Today there are more social networking account than there are people on the planet_

2. Underline the background information. What information does it provide to help readers understand what will follow? _More detail of social media_

3. Underline the thesis statement. Based on the thesis statement, what do you think the essay will be about? _Social media can be dangerous_

4. What is the topic of the thesis statement? _~~The risk~~ social media can be dangerous_

5. What is the controlling idea of the thesis statement? _Social media is dangerous_

Rhetorical Focus

Body Paragraphs
The **body paragraphs** contain the **supporting details** of the essay.

- The **topic sentence** clearly states the content of each paragraph. It supports and expands on an aspect of the **topic** and **controlling idea** of the essay's **thesis statement.** The topic sentence is often the first sentence of a body paragraph.

- Each body paragraph must develop a point presented in the topic statement. All the supporting details in a body paragraph must clearly relate to each other. They can be descriptions, definitions, examples, anecdotes, statistics, or quotations. Quotations may come from a published work or from a personal interview.

- The **concluding sentence** may either bring the idea of the paragraph to a close or suggest the content of the next paragraph.

Exercise 4 Examining body paragraphs

Examine the body paragraphs of the essay, "Becoming an Academic Writer," on pages 3–4. Then respond to the questions and statements below. Compare your answers with a partner.

Body Paragraph 1

1. Circle the topic sentence.

2. What supporting details does the writer give? How do these details support the topic sentence? _personal experience and science, use example to support_

3. The concluding sentence _____
   a. brings the idea of the paragraph to a close.
   b. suggests the content of the next paragraph.

Body Paragraph 2

1. Circle the topic sentence.

2. What supporting details does the writer provide? How do these details support the topic sentence? _professor doesn't recognize him, use example to support_

3. The concluding sentence _____
   a. brings the idea of the paragraph to a close.
   b. suggests the content of the next paragraph.

Body Paragraph 3

1. Circle the topic sentence.

2. What supporting details does the writer provide? How do these details support the topic sentence? _slang and abbreviated term, use example to support_

3. The concluding sentence _____
   a. brings the idea of the paragraph to a close.
   b. suggests the content of the next paragraph.

Rhetorical Focus

The Conclusion
Academic essays end with a **conclusion** that brings the essay to a close.

- The conclusion is usually two to four sentences in length.
- It restates the essay's thesis in different words. This restatement connects the conclusion to the introduction.
- It may give advice or a warning.
- It may make a prediction or ask a question.
- It can provide new insights and discoveries that the writer has gained.

Exercise 5 Examining a conclusion

Reread the conclusion of "Becoming an Academic Writer" from page 4. Then respond to the questions and statements below.

> Academic writing requires critical thinking skills, an understanding of the topic, research, high-level vocabulary, and correct grammar. Having these skills is empowering since it has made me a better communicator and student. I have come a long way since I started college, and I am now proud of the writing that I produce.

1. How many sentences appear in the conclusion?

    3

2. Underline the sentence in the conclusion that restates the thesis in the introduction.
3. The conclusion ends with _____
    a. some advice.   c. a warning.
    b. a prediction.   d. an insight.

In **Writing Process Part 2** you will . . .

- learn how to analyze an assignment.
- learn how to select and narrow a topic.
- learn how to research a topic.
- learn to collect information from both primary and secondary sources.

Critical Thinking Focus

Understanding Assignments

When you get a writing assignment, read it carefully to gain a full understanding of your task before you get started. Look for the following information:

Topic　　　　　What will your writing be about?

Purpose　　　　What is your goal? Will you inform, entertain, explain, or persuade?

Audience　　　Who will read your essay? What will they expect? What relationship do you have with these readers? How formal should your writing be?

Rhetorical Mode　Are you being asked to compare and contrast ideas, provide causes or effects, argue an opinion, classify, or react to something?

Style or Format　Will you write in a specific style? What font size will you use?

Length　　　　How long will your essay be?

Due Date　　　When do you need to hand in the finished essay?

It might help to annotate these directly into the assignment. Circle or underline and write pointers to each important element in the assignment. In this way, you will see the information quickly when you refer back to the assignment.

Topic

Many large cities worldwide are **restricting the use of automobiles**. In fact, some countries like Germany have closed off streets to cars completely, and others have limited vehicular traffic to specific times of the day. Write an article for **an environmental magazine** in which you **explain the effects of this policy on society**. What are some reasons for implementing this course of action? To meet the deadline, the article must be received by **April 14th**. Write **no more than three pages, double-spaced, using a 12-point Times New Roman font and a 1-inch margin**.

Audience — Purpose — Rhetorical Mode — Length — Format — Due Date

Refer back to your assignment frequently as you research and write each draft of your essay. You will want to be sure that you have met all of your instructor's expectations.

Exercise 1 Understanding your assignment

Read the writing task. Then respond to the questions and statements below.

> Many books are adapted as films. Sometimes a film is quite different from the book. The directors have to make choices about which parts of the story will transfer best to the screen. Write a movie review for a newspaper. Compare a book that you have read with its movie version. In what ways are they similar? How are they different? Write four pages, double-spaced, using a 12-point Times New Roman font and a 1-inch margin.

1. What is the topic? _____
2. Who is the audience? _____
3. Underline the style and format.

Critical Thinking Focus

Words Used to Signal Rhetorical Modes
Clues about the essay's **rhetorical mode** are often written into the assignment as **signal words.** Take a look at the signal words in the chart below.

SIGNAL WORDS	RHETORICAL MODES
similarities, differences, contrast, like, unlike, same, different	Comparison-Contrast Essay
consequences, results, outcomes, reasons, factors	Cause-and-Effect Essay
against, agree, argue, disagree, defend, position, convince, prove	Argumentative Essay
categorize, classify, types, rank	Classification Essay
analyze, critique, interpret, evaluate	Reaction Essay

Each unit of this book focuses on one rhetorical mode.
- In Unit 2, you will learn to write comparison-contrast essays.
- In Unit 3, you will learn to write cause-and-effect essays.
- In Unit 4, you will learn to write argumentative essays.
- In Unit 5, you will learn to write classification essays.
- In Unit 6, you will learn to write reaction essays.

Exercise 2 Identifying the rhetorical mode

Reread the assignment in Exercise 1 on page 10. Then answer the following questions.

1. What is the rhetorical mode? _____

   _____

2. How do you know? _____

   _____

   _____

Exercise 3 Identifying signal words and rhetorical modes

Read the assignment. Then respond to the question and statement below.

> Some universities are deciding whether or not to eliminate their physical education requirement for graduation. Faculty members are asking students for their input. Write an essay for the school faculty arguing in favor or against this requirement. Defend your position with strong evidence including statistics, examples, and research from reliable sources. Some of your readers may not agree with your point of view. Counter their objections with strong evidence that will convince them of your position.

1. Circle any words that signal the rhetorical mode.

2. What is the rhetorical mode? _____

Rhetorical Focus

Selecting and Narrowing a Topic

When selecting a topic for research, it is important to limit your subject area.

Once you have decided on your subject (or are given a subject), for example the Middle Ages, make a list of what you already know.

Look the subject up in an encyclopedia to get an overview of the subject. Then list aspects that interest you most.

Review different media sources (books, journals, and websites) to narrow your subject to one specific topic, such as music in the Middle Ages. The more specific your topic is, the easier it will be to focus on the relevant information.

Narrow the topic even further, such as Italian music in the Middle Ages or Italian music in the late Middle Ages.

Respond to the prompts below.

1. Make a list of what you know on the subject of space exploration.

   _____

   _____

   _____

2. Look up space exploration in an encyclopedia to get an overview of the subject. Then list aspects that interest you.

   _____

   _____

   _____

3. Narrow the subject by choosing one aspect of space exploration. Write the topic below.

   _____

   _____

   _____

Rhetorical Focus

Collecting Information from Primary and Secondary Sources

Libraries, government offices, museums, and the Internet provide a wealth of reliable sources. You may also want to interview people or send emails to experts on your topic. As you conduct research, use both **primary** and **secondary** sources.

Primary Sources

Primary sources are original materials such as legal documents, artifacts, letters, interviews, or speeches. These sources give first-hand accounts of history and historical records.

Secondary Sources

Secondary sources have been analyzed and/or explained by a third party. They include textbooks, third-person magazine articles, and scholarly journals.

Whether you use primary or secondary sources, you must determine just how objective each source is to be sure the writers do not have a bias that will negatively affect your credibility.

Identifying primary and secondary sources

Classify the following sources as primary or secondary sources. If the source can fall into both categories, write it in both places.

autobiographies	diaries	email
encyclopedia articles	museum exhibits	oral histories
scientific magazine articles	textbooks	

PRIMARY SOURCES	SECONDARY SOURCES
autobiographies	

Rhetorical Focus

Guidelines for Researching a Topic

Once you have a topic, such as Italian music in the Middle Ages, and are ready to begin your research, follow these steps:

• Scan websites and articles to become familiar with Italian music during the Middle Ages.

• Develop research questions based on your findings.

Who were the most famous Italian composers during the Middle Ages?

What types of instruments did they play?

• Use only reliable sources such as historical records, scholarly journals, highly respected national newspapers, university publications, and websites from respected institutions.

• Avoid unreliable sources found in popular magazines, anonymous Internet articles, blogs, tabloid publications, or advertising.

• Take notes by reading through articles, and highlight important points that relate to your thesis. Your notes should include information about the source such as the title, author, publication, date, page numbers, and URL. This information will help you remember where you got your information in case you want to refer back to it. Also, you will need some of this information when you cite your sources in your essays.

Exercise 6 Conducting research

Think about a topic you would like to write about. Then answer the following questions with that topic in mind.

1. Where will you go first to begin your research?

_____

_____

2. How can you tell the difference between reliable and unreliable sources?

_____

_____

3. What are some reliable sources you will look for when you do research?

_____

_____

4. How will you organize your notes so that you can refer back to them as you write?

_____

_____

 In **Writing Process Part 3** you will . . .

- learn about unity within paragraphs and essays.
- learn about coherence.
- learn strategies for achieving coherence in your writing.

Rhetorical Focus

Unity

Effective writing must have **unity**. Unity occurs when all the ideas in a paragraph or an essay support each other.

Unity within a Paragraph

A paragraph has unity when all the sentences support the topic sentence, the main idea of the paragraph. Without unity, the paragraph loses focus. The topic sentence of the paragraph should focus on **one** topic and controlling idea. The supporting details of the paragraph must support the topic sentence. If they do not, they will be irrelevant and confuse readers.

The paragraph below contains sentences that do not support the topic and controlling idea expressed in the topic sentence. These irrelevant sentences have been crossed out to preserve unity.

> Septimus Harding was my favorite character in the novel *Barchester Towers* by Anthony Trollope. ~~This novel is part of the series called the Chronicles of Barsetshire.~~ Some of the qualities I valued most in him were his devotion to his daughter and his generosity of spirit. Even though he believed that his daughter was going to marry a man that Harding didn't admire, Harding respected his daughter's choice. ~~Eleanor Bold was a very strong willed woman.~~ Also, he gave up a coveted position to another job candidate because the man had twelve children and needed the money. ~~*Barchester Towers*, published in 1857, is about the prominent citizens in a small city in England.~~ Unfortunately, many other characters in the novel felt they could take advantage of Harding's gentle nature.

Exercise 1 Editing for unity

Read the two paragraphs below. Draw a line through the sentences that are irrelevant. The first one is done for you. There are six more.

> Having my friends and family together at my wedding was an amazing experience. I had not seen some of my aunts, uncles, and cousins for many years. ~~My cousin Tom lives in London, where he works as an engineer.~~ My mother was born in Spain, and my father was born in Indonesia, so my relatives are scattered all over the world. I ~~really like traveling, and I have been to Europe and Asia to visit relatives.~~ Although my family tries to get together for important occasions, this was the first time everyone

could attend. I felt so honored that it was my wedding that brought us all together. ~~It was also important to introduce my friends and my new husband to my relatives. All these years, none of my friends had met my relatives. Developing good friendships takes a lot of work.~~ Watching my family, friends, and new husband all dancing, laughing, and having a wonderful time together will stay in my memory forever.

The band we hired played music that the guests loved, and we danced for hours. ~~My original guest list had over 200 people, but I had to cut it down to 150.~~ It was difficult finding a group that could play all the diverse styles that my husband and I wanted at the wedding. Most bands specialize in one or two different kinds of music. However, these musicians really knew all types of music—from 1940s jazz and swing, to salsa, merengue, and even tango. ~~My brother was once in a band.~~ In short, there was music to suit everyone's tastes. ~~I loved the singer's beautiful blue dress. It was incredible.~~ Even my grandparents danced all night.

Rhetorical Focus

Unity within an Essay

An essay has unity when all the body paragraphs contain a topic sentence and supporting sentences that reinforce the thesis of the essay. Without unity, the essay loses focus and goes off topic.

In the example below, topic sentences 1 and 2 both support the thesis statement. However, notice how topic sentence 3 goes off topic.

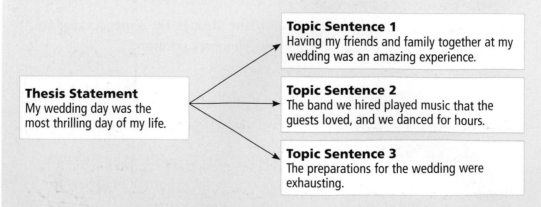

Thesis Statement
My wedding day was the most thrilling day of my life.

Topic Sentence 1
Having my friends and family together at my wedding was an amazing experience.

Topic Sentence 2
The band we hired played music that the guests loved, and we danced for hours.

Topic Sentence 3
The preparations for the wedding were exhausting.

Although topic sentence 3 is still about the wedding, it does not support the idea that the wedding day was thrilling.

Exercise 2 Recognizing unity within an essay

Read the following thesis statements. Put a check (✓) next to each topic sentence that supports the thesis statement.

1. **Thesis:** After two years of job hunting, I have finally found the perfect job for me.
   Topic Sentences:
   ___✓___ a. I am enthusiastic about the challenges that I confront at work every day.
   ___✓___ b. Last year I almost got a good job.
   ___✓___ c. I am making more money than I have ever made, and I have so many benefits.
   ___✓___ d. My boss is very supportive, and she is helping me to succeed.
   ___✓___ e. I did not like the job that I had before.

2. **Thesis:** Skiing is a great sport, but it is not for everyone.
   Topic Sentences:
   ___✓___ a. Not everyone has the ability to ski well.
   ___✓___ b. Becoming a good skier means taking certain risks that some people are afraid to take.
   ___✓___ c. Skiing is more difficult than ice-skating.
   ___✓___ d. A day on the slopes is not always affordable for everyone.
   _____ e. Skiing down the highest slope can be dangerous.

Rheforical Focus

Coherence
Coherence in a paragraph means that all the ideas fit together in a logical flow. In a coherent paragraph, the relationship between ideas is clear, and one idea connects logically to the next. Coherence can be achieved by using transitions, logical order, pronouns, and parallel forms.

Using Transitions for Coherence
Transitions show how one idea relates to another. The transition *however* serves to set up two contrasting ideas.

   She likes to read novels. **However,** she does not enjoy biographies.

Transitions are separated from the rest of the sentence by **commas**.

   I enjoy writing in my journal. **However,** I do not like writing letters.
   I enjoy writing in my journal. I do not like writing letters, **however.**

Transitions can be used with a **semicolon** and a comma to form a compound sentence.

   His first novel was not a success; **however,** his second work became a bestseller.

semi colon
(顺号)

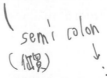

Below is a list of some transitions and their use.

Use	Transitions
Example	for instance, to demonstrate, for example, in some cases
Additional Idea	moreover, furthermore, in addition
Contrast	however, in contrast, on the contrary, nevertheless, nonetheless, whereas, even though, although, unlike
Similarities	similarly, likewise
Cause	as a result, therefore, thus, consequently
Emphasis	indeed, in fact, obviously
Result	therefore, consequently
Conclusion	in conclusion, in summary

Exercise 3 Identifying coherence

One sentence is missing from each short paragraph below. Choose the sentence that best completes the paragraph.

In many ways the invention of email and computers has led to the decline of traditional letter writing. Email makes it easier to get in touch with faraway friends. _____ For these reasons fewer people are sending letters through the postal service.

    a. I bought a new computer last week.

    (b.) Furthermore, email is convenient and essentially free.

Audio books have become very popular in our fast-paced society. One of the reasons is that people do not have the time to sit still and read. _____ Some listen while jogging outdoors or exercising in the gym. Therefore, an audio book makes for a great gift idea for the active book lover.

    a. Stephen King published a book in this format.

    b. In fact, many people listen to these books while driving to and from work.

Don Quixote de la Mancha is an epic novel written in the 1600s by Miguel de Cervantes. This is the story of a man who read so many books on chivalry and knighthood that he went crazy. _____ Together they had many adventures while searching for truth and beauty and upholding the highest ideals.

    a. He traveled the world as a ridiculous knight along with his friend, Sancho Panza.

    b. Don Quixote came from a small town in Spain called La Mancha.

Exercise 4 Using transitions

Combine the following sentences to create coherence by using transitions from the box.

| in contrast   nevertheless   previously   therefore   for example   moreover |

1. I want to study in Italy for a year to learn about art. I enrolled in Italian classes.

   I want to study in Italy for a year to learn about art. Therefore, I enrolled in Italian classes.

2. Learning a foreign language takes a lot of patience and effort. It helps to have a good ear.

   Learning a foreign language takes a lot of ~~patience and effort~~. Moreover, it helps to have a good ear,

3. The college student was told to revise her essay a third time. She has made great progress with her writing skills.

   The college student was told to revise her essay a third time. Nevertheless, she has made great progress with her writing skills.

4. John Steinbeck, a famous American author, wrote many books concerning the human condition. His novel *The Grapes of Wrath* dealt with the problems of the Great Depression.

   John Steinbeck, a famous American author, wrote many books concerning the human condition. For example, his novel The Grapes of Wrath dealt with the problems of the Great Depression,

5. Academic writing requires a knowledge of standard grammar, sophisticated vocabulary, and proper organization. Electronic text messages use abbreviations, symbols, and slang.

   Academic writing requires a knowledge of standard grammer, sophisticated vocabulary, and proper organization. In contrast, electronic text message use abbreviations symbols, and slang.

6. Nowadays research is often done on the Internet. Important information was stored on special film called microfiche.

   Nowadays research is often done on the Internet. Previously important information was stored on special film called microfiche.

Ordering Ideas for Coherence

One way to achieve coherence in an essay is to arrange ideas in a logical order, such as **chronological order** or **order of importance**.

When arranging ideas in chronological order, use language such as *in the beginning, first, second, next, then,* or *finally.*

> **First**, I went to the bank. **Next**, I visited my mother in the hospital.

When arranging ideas in order of importance, order items from the most important to the least important or vice versa. Use language such *as the most/least important thing, the next priority,* or *the third/final priority/goal.*

> **The most important thing** for me was to understand the assignment before beginning my research.

Exercise 5 Ordering ideas in a paragraph

A. Use the list of ideas to write a short paragraph. Arrange your ideas in chronological order. Use language from the Rhetorical Focus box above. The first sentence has been done for you.

- develop a questionnaire
- interview participants
- analyze the data

If you want to conduct a survey, first develop a questionnaire.

_____

_____

_____

B. Use the list of ideas to write a short paragraph. Arrange your ideas in order of importance. Use language from the Rhetorical Focus box above.

- practice speaking Spanish with friends
- take a Spanish class
- visit a Spanish-speaking country

There are several ways to learn Spanish, such as practicing speaking Spanish with friends, taking a Spanish class, or visiting a Spanish-speaking country. Learning Spanish need patient and step by step. First, taking a Spanish class. Then, tring to practice with friends. Last, visiting a spanish-speaking

Rhetorical Focus

Using Pronoun Reference for Coherence

A **pronoun** can replace a noun. *I, you, he, it, this, that, those,* and *these* are examples of pronouns. Pronouns can create coherence in an essay.

What is <u>revision</u> and why is **it** necessary?

Pronouns can also replace whole phrases or ideas.

<u>I left my expensive dictionary in the library</u>. I do not know how I did **that**.

Pronouns must agree in number and gender with the noun they refer to.

I have a younger <u>brother</u>. He is a lawyer.

x I have a younger brother. She is a lawyer. (incorrect)

Exercise 6 Identifying pronoun reference

Read the paragraph. Choose the correct pronoun to complete each sentence.

On Sunday afternoon, my mother and I went to visit my grandfather. I was looking forward to seeing (him / her) again. Unfortunately, my sister
1.
Diana and my father were unable to go because (they / he) had to work
2.
that weekend. My mother and I drove to my grandfather's house. When
(we / I) arrived, my aunt and my grandfather greeted (us / we) at the door.
3.   **4.**
(They / She) were very excited to see (us / it).
5.   **6.**

Rhetorical Focus

Using Parallel Forms for Coherence

Another strategy to achieve coherence is to use **parallel forms**.
This means that all items in a list have the same grammatical form.

I like **playing** tennis, **swimming**, and **dancing**.

x I like playing tennis, swimming, and to dance. (INCORRECT)

She **cooked** dinner, **set** the table, and **arranged** the flowers.

x She cooked dinner, set the table, and the flowers were arranged. (INCORRECT)

Exercise 7 Using parallel forms

Rewrite the following sentences to correct the nonparallel forms.

1. At the age of twenty, I started to write plays, taking acting lessons, and produce shows.

   <u>At the age of twenty, I started to write plays, take acting lessons,</u>

   <u>and produce shows.</u>

2. As a teenager, I reported on school events, editing articles for the high school newspaper, and published some of my stories.

   _____

   _____

3. Some of the rewards of being an author are learn about historical events, researching the lives of famous people, and discovering facts about yourself.

   _____

   _____

4. Attending workshops on writing has taught me how to receive criticism, became a more focused writer, and taking more risks.

   _____

   _____

In **Writing Process Part 4** you will . . .

- learn about main and dependent clauses.
- learn how to correct run-ons and sentence fragments.
- learn about verb tense consistency.

Editing involves making changes to your writing to improve it and to correct mistakes.

Language and Grammar Focus

Clauses

Every clause in English must have a subject and a verb. There are two types of clauses: **main clauses** and **dependent clauses.**

Main Clauses

A main clause contains a complete idea and can stand alone as a sentence.

I read my speech at graduation.

Dependent Clauses

A dependent clause does not contain a complete idea and cannot stand alone as a complete sentence. A dependent clause often starts with a **subordinating conjunction** such as *after, before, although, because, since, when,* or *while.* A dependent clause can be attached to a main clause to form a **complex sentence.** A dependent clause can come before or after the main clause.

When the dependent clause begins the sentence, place a **comma** after it.

| dependent clause | | main clause |

When I read my speech at graduation, all my friends and family were amazed.

When the independent clause comes at the end of the sentence, omit the comma.

| main clause | | dependent clause |

All my friends and family were amazed **when I read my speech at graduation.**

Exercise 1 Identifying main and dependent clauses

Circle the main clause and underline the dependent clause in each sentence. Add punctuation if necessary.

1. When I came into the auditorium, the room was empty.

2. I felt very confident because I had spent a long time practicing.

3. Since it was my graduation I bought a beautiful new outfit.

4. Although the ceremony was very long nobody was bored.

5. We went out for a fancy meal after the ceremony ended.

6. My family took a lot of photographs which I still enjoy looking at.

Language and Grammar Focus

Run-on Sentences

Run-on sentences are incorrect. Run-on sentence errors occur when two main clauses occur together with no connector or incorrect punctuation between them.

x Mario Vargas Llosa is a Nobel Prize-winning writer he also ran for president of Peru. (INCORRECT)

Run-on sentence errors can also occur when two main clauses are separated by a comma.

x Mario Vargas Llosa is a Nobel Prize-winning writer, he also ran for president of Peru. (INCORRECT)

A run-on sentence can be corrected in several ways.

- You can change one of the main clauses to a dependent clause by adding a **subordinating conjunction** such as *because, when, before,* or *although.*

   Although Mario Vargas Llosa is best known as a Nobel Prize-winning writer, he also ran for president of Peru.

- You can use a **coordinating conjunction** such as *and, but, yet, or, so,* or *for* to connect two clauses and to form a **compound sentence**. Use a **comma** before the coordinating conjunction.

   Mario Vargas Llosa is a Nobel Prize-winning writer, **but** he also ran for president of Peru.

- You can also use punctuation to correct a run-on sentence. Use a **period** between two main clauses that contain two separate and distinct ideas. Use a **semicolon** between the clauses that are very close in meaning.

   Mario Vargas Llosa is a Nobel Prize-winning writer. He also ran for president of Peru.

   Mario Vargas Llosa is a Nobel Prize-winning writer; his books have been translated into more than thirty languages.

Exercise 2 Identifying run-on sentences

Write *RO* next to the run-on sentences and *C* next to the correct sentences.

  RO 1. My family and I came from Vietnam I was 16 years old.

_____ 2. Ramya visited Mexico she did not know Spanish.

_____ 3. Because I did not know how to use a computer, I was worried about my job skills.

_____ 4. People are very busy working they do not have time to study.

_____ 5. Since I now know how to drive, I can take my sister to school.

_____ 6. Smart phones are good for sending email, they can also be used as cameras.

Exercise 3 Using coordinating conjunctions to correct run-on sentences

Use a coordinating conjunction from the box to correct each run-on sentence.
You may use some coordinating conjunctions more than once.

and	but	so	or	yet	for

fanboy on route → coordinating parte conjunction

1. The great American author Mark Twain traveled a lot, he still made time for his daughter.

   <u>The great American author Mark Twain traveled a lot, but he still made</u>
   <u>time for his daughter.</u>

2. Jabra Ibrahim Jabra translated many books and poems into Arabic, *and* his literary criticism has enlightened his audience.

   _____

   _____

3. Isabel Allende wanted to chronicle the founding of Santiago, Chile, *or* *so* she wrote *Inez of My Soul.*

   _____

   _____

4. Jane Austen's original version of *Pride and Prejudice* was written when she *but* was only twenty years old, it was not published for almost two decades.

   _____

   _____

5. Jhumpa Lahiri writes about Indians living far from home, *and* she won the Pulitzer Prize for her book *Interpreter of Maladies.*

   _____

   _____

6. Writers often use autobiographical information to write fiction, *and* they adapt the background of other people for their stories.

   _____

   _____

Exercise 4 Using subordinating conjunctions to correct run-on sentences

Use one of the following subordinating conjunctions to correct each run-on sentence.

although	since	when	because

1. Ernest Hemingway wrote about the lost generation after World War I, he was living in Paris. _When Ernest Hemingway wrote about the lost generation after World War I, he was living in Paris._

2. Umberto Eco was able to write the novel *The Name of the Rose*, *because* he was knowledgeable about the Medieval period and philosophy. _____

3. René Prudhomme was an engineer by profession *although* he won the first Nobel Prize for Literature for his poetry and essays. _____

4. Many of Tolstoy's epic novels have been made into movies *since* they have unforgettable characters. _____

5. Gabriel García Márquez gave up his law studies *when* he actively pursued a career in writing. _____

Language and Grammar Focus

Sentence Fragments

A **sentence fragment** is an error because it cannot stand by itself; it is a dependent clause. It may have a subject and a verb, but it needs a main clause to complete a thought. Look at the sentence fragment below.

x When I first started college. (INCORRECT)

Avoid sentence fragments by ensuring that each dependent clause follows or precedes a main clause.

dependent clause		main clause

When I first started college, I was excited about facing new challenges.

main clause	dependent clause

She found out **because I told her.**

Exercise 5 Correcting sentence fragments

Rewrite each sentence fragment as a correct sentence by adding a main clause. Compare your answers with a partner.

1. Although we do not see each other very often.

   <u>Although we do not see each other very often, my sister and I always</u>

   <u>stay in touch.</u>

2. When I visited her.

   <u>When I visited her, she was taking a nap.</u>

3. Because she had a demanding job.

   <u>Because she had a demanding job, she commited</u>

   <u>suicide.</u>

4. Since I was her favorite.

   <u>Since I was her favorite, she gave me lots of money.</u>

5. After she got married.

   <u>After she got married, she died.</u>

GO ONLINE

Language and Grammar Focus

Verb Tense Consistency

When writing an essay, it is important to be consistent in the use of verbs. If you are not consistent, your readers might misunderstand your ideas.

When describing facts and habits, use the simple present.

> Tourists **visit** the Taj Mahal and **enjoy** its history and beauty.

When telling a story, use the simple past.

> On our trip to Peru, we **visited** Machu Picchu and **toured** the ancient ruins of the Inca civilization.

You may only shift from the simple past to the simple present if there is a logical reason for doing so. Look at the example below. The writer shifts from the simple past to the simple present to make a comparison between the past and the present.

> In the 15th century, the Taj Mahal **was built** as a memorial to Shah Jahan's wife. However, today it **is** a popular tourist attraction.

Read the paragraph. Find and correct seven more mistakes in verb consistency.

While I was visiting China, I experience^d a special kind of warmth from
the people I come in contact with. I was always aware of their special
quality of friendliness. I have the unique experience of being in Beijing
on the night the Chinese win their bid to host the 2008 summer Olympics.
On that night, I am one of a million and a half people who poured into
the streets to express their joy and gratitude. I walked with them and shake
hands with as many people as I could while I sang out the words: "gong
xi ni ba" (congratulations). My words are always met with big smiles
and enthusiastic handshakes. Those parents with kids on their shoulders,
teenagers, and many others feel as if the rest of the world was welcoming
them into the global community. Now I wish them the best, and I hope to
return one day. If you take a trip to China, you will experience the same
kind of hospitality.

In **Review** you will . . .

- review how to understand your writing assignment.
- practice identifying primary and secondary sources.
- review the elements of an introduction and a conclusion.
- review unity and coherence.

In Putting It All Together you will review the concepts you learned in this unit.

Exercise 1 Understanding your assignment

Read the writing task. Then respond to the questions and statements below.

> Both European and Indian music have flourished throughout the centuries. Take on the role of a music critic and compare European classical music with Indian classical music. Consider the origins, characteristics, rhythm, tone, and instruments used in both musical traditions. In your analysis, illustrate how the melody and scales influence each tradition. Write six pages, double-spaced, using a 12-point Times New Roman font and a one-inch margin.

1. Circle the topic.

2. What is the rhetorical mode?_____

3. What research would this assignment require? _____

4. Underline the format and length of the essay.

Exercise 2 Identifying primary and secondary sources

Classify the following sources into primary and secondary sources. Some sources fit in both categories.

biographies	documentaries	marriage licenses	magazine articles
newsletters	photographs	screenplays	surveys

PRIMARY SOURCES	SECONDARY SOURCES

Exercise 3 Examining an introduction

Read this essay introduction. Then respond to the questions and statements below.

Overcoming a Difficult Situation

Difficult life-changing experiences become the memories that stay forever in our minds. We have to learn to balance the positive and negative effects that these situations have on us. The day after I finished my first year at college, I had one of these life-changing experiences. A mishap on my way to a job interview at an international bank taught me an important lesson.

[handwritten annotations: "include reader", "mistake happen"]

1. Circle the hook.

2. Find the background information and write it below. _The day after I finished my first year at college, I had one of these life-changing experience._

3. Underline the thesis statement.

4. Write the topic of the thesis statement. _A mishap taught me an important lesson._

5. Write the controlling idea of the thesis statement. _on my way to a job interview at an international bank_

Exercise 4 Reordering for coherence

The following sentences make up body paragraph 1 of "Overcoming a Difficult Situation." Number them from 1 to 7 to show logical time order.

___ a. Of course I was very happy to hear the news, but I was also nervous.

___ b. It all started the day I received an unexpected phone call.

___ c. I knew that arriving late would give a negative impression and would show that I was irresponsible.

___ d. She wanted to set up a job interview with me.

___ e. The following week, on the day of the interview, I was so excited that I had a hard time deciding what clothes to wear.

___ f. It was from the manager of a very important financial institution.

___ g. I had to really hurry once I was dressed because I did not want to arrive late.

Exercise 5 **Editing paragraphs for coherence**

A. Read body paragraph 2 of "Overcoming a Difficult Situation," and edit as necessary. There are seven mistakes with run-on sentences and sentence fragments.

I was in a rush to get there, I decided to take a taxi. The traffic was so horrible that the driver was in a bad mood. He closed the door, my new skirt got caught. I tried desperately to pull it out, but it ripped. I thought about asking the driver to stop, I was too embarrassed to say anything. Although I was very upset. I tried to be calm. The ride was much longer than I expected, the air conditioning was not working. I did not want anything negative to block my mind I was eager to have this job. I wanted to have a good interview and make a strong impression. Since I learned in school that first impressions are the most valuable.

B. Read body paragraph 3 of "Overcoming a Difficult Situation," and edit as necessary. There are eight mistakes with verb tense.

Finally when I arrived at the bank, I look at my skirt. The torn hem was hanging and was covered with dirt. Once inside, I go into the ladies room. I tried to wash my skirt and hold it together with a safety pin. A few minutes later, I was in the waiting room when the secretary call me. I was embarrassed and afraid that I would not get the job because of my sloppy appearance. The most interesting part was that the manager asked me what happen. When I tell her the story, she started to laugh. She can't stop. She wanted to ask me something about myself, but she keeps on laughing. Now I was sure I would not get the job. She said, "I will never forget this. I never thought that I will have such a good time today. You know, when you have to interview a lot of people in one day, it can become very boring." Despite this ordeal, she assured me that I had the right qualifications, and in the end she offered me the position.

Exercise 6 Examining a conclusion

Read the conclusion of "Overcoming a Difficult Situation." Then respond to the statements below.

> I remember this experience because it taught me to be prepared and on time but to also stay calm and persevere. In fact, everything that happened on that one day gave me the confidence to go forward and achieve my goals in the company. We never know when a negative experience can have a positive influence on our lives.

1. Underline the sentence in the conclusion that restates the thesis from the introduction.
2. The conclusion ends with _____.
   a. some advice.   c. a warning.
   b. a prediction.   d. an insight.

Exercise 7 Identifying pronoun reference

Read the paragraphs. Choose the correct pronoun to complete each sentence.

   Many people I know want attention, love, or recognition from others. Some of (they / **them**) get frustrated because they do not achieve what they want. In my case, I wanted recognition, and I got (**it** / him) from writing. From age thirteen, I had always imagined that one day I would write short stories and become a well-known author. When I was at college, I had a good friend—Jessica Bardwell. Jessica was majoring in English composition, and (her / **she**) encouraged me to take a creative writing class. I did, and (they / **it**) helped me improve my writing style enormously.

   Jessica would also often accompany me to poetry readings and writing workshops. Anybody could get up and present his or her work, so I decided to present (**mine** / my). It was great! My classmates really

helped (I / me) to feel confident about my writing. Then, close to my
6.
graduation, the college English Department invited all of (we / us)
7.
to participate in a poetry contest. My poem "Fragments of a Life" won

first prize and appeared in the local newspaper. (This / These) was
8.
the beginning of my professional career as a writer. I could not have

accomplished what I did without Jessica's help. I have learned from

this experience that anyone can dream, but it is much easier to achieve

a goal with a friend.

Exercise 8 Using transitions for coherence

Combine the following sentences to create coherence by using transitions from
the box.

in contrast	nevertheless	therefore	for example	moreover

1. Sometimes when essays are written too quickly, the sentences do not flow naturally.
   You should always read your essay out loud to make sure it sounds natural.

   _____

   _____

2. The sonnets of Shakespeare always rhyme. Modern poetry usually uses free verse
   that does not rhyme.

   _____

   _____

3. Writing a good play requires a strong story line. You need realistic dialogue and
   believable characters.

   _____

   _____

4. William Shakespeare wrote comedies as well as tragedies. *The Taming of the Shrew* and *A Midsummer Night's Dream* both have happy endings.

_____

_____

5. Word-processing programs can check grammar and spelling. A good writer should not depend on these tools.

_____

_____

Exercise 9 Using parallel forms

Rewrite the following sentences to correct the nonparallel forms.

1. A few years ago, I went to China to research a book, meet some old friends, and visiting the famous temples.

___*visit*_____

_____

2. One day we toured the Ming Dynasty gardens, walked through the narrow streets, and were visiting the Great Wall.

___*visited*_____

_____

3. I was eating with chopsticks, sampled spicy foods, and drank exotic teas.

_____*sampling*_____*drinking*_____

_____

4. The Chinese are famous for creating silk screens, paint lacquer boxes, and inventing calligraphy.

_____*painting*_____

_____

5. I enrolled in a Chinese culture class where I learned how to write a few characters, spoke a few words, and recognize the different tones of the language.

___*speak*_____

_____

UNIT 2

Comparison-Contrast Essays

Unit Goals

Critical Thinking Focus

- comparison and contrast signal words

Research Focus

- using search engines
- evaluating reliability of sources

Rhetorical Focus

- comparison-contrast organization

Language and Grammar Focus

- prepositional phrases
- restrictive and nonrestrictive relative clauses

People sometimes walk through life without taking the time to observe the world around them. A good photograph can both capture a piece of the world and elicit strong reactions from the viewer. In this unit, you will compare and contrast two photographs that share at least one common element.

Mother and Daughter Flying a Kite

Father and Son Fixing a Bicycle

Exercise 1 Thinking about the topic

A. Discuss the pictures with a partner.

- What is happening in these pictures?
- How are the children reacting to the experiences?
- How do you think the adults in these pictures feel?
- Can you remember a similar experience? How did you feel?

B. Make notes about what makes an individual photograph memorable to you. Then discuss in small groups.

In the first picture, there are two handsome guy exchange football shirts. And one of shirts is the boy in the second picture wear. Both of them are serious seems like it is an vital thing for them. Therefore, the reasonable situation is the guy get yellow shirt is a boss of a football club, buying a player who take red shirt.
The difference between two pictures is one is indoor and one is outdoor. It seem like it is a comfortable temperature in former one and hot in later.

This article by Randy Kennedy explains why some medical schools are offering courses in art appreciation. How can looking at art improve the observation skills of medical students?

At Some Medical Schools, Humanities Join the Curriculum

Art and medicine have worked **hand in hand** for a long time. To improve his art, Leonardo dissected bodies. To improve his anatomy treatise, Andreas Vesalius relied on the artistry of Titian's workshop.

But the other day, in the European paintings **wing** of the Metropolitan Museum of Art, a group of seven would-be doctors had a different kind of reason to appreciate a 17th-century Dutch scene before them: course credit. Three years ago, the Mount Sinai School of Medicine began an art-appreciation course for medical students, joining a growing number of medical schools that are adding humanities to the usual forced march of physiology, pathology, and microbiology.

This year, for the first time, the course is required for third-year students, providing them not only with a blinking-into-the-sun break from medical **rotations** but also, said Dr. David Muller, the school's chairman of medical education, a lesson about how important, and **underrated**, the art of looking is to the practice of medicine. "To make a better doctor means to me one who sees the person and not just the patient," he said.

One study, published in *the Journal of the American Medical Association* in 2001, has found that looking at painting and sculpture can improve medical students' observational abilities.

It could also, wrote Dr. Irwin Braverman, a Yale medical professor and an author of the study, eventually reduce health-care costs. "With heightened observational skills," he wrote, "physicians can often ask the questions necessary to make correct diagnoses without relying too much on costly blood tests and X-rays."

Rebecca Hirschwerk, an art educator who is the course's instructor and one of its creators along with Dr. Muller, began to think about how, in listening and poring over charts, doctors sometimes had little time actually to look at their patients, especially under the pressures of today's managed medical care.

"I can't think of many places outside art where you can be in a moment, and just look, for as long as you can take it," she said. "Think about what it would be like if you were with a patient and could freeze the moment to really pay attention to everything that patient was trying to tell you. It's hard to do when you have only 15 minutes with patients, 20 times a day."

On one particular museum visit, Ms. Hirschwerk asked the students to study *The Proposal* by the 19th-century French painter Adolphe-William Bouguereau for several minutes and then to turn away from it and recall the painting's details, which they did in great detail, from the cat sitting at the woman's feet to the almost invisible **strand** of thread stretched between her fingers.

Dr. Muller said that students were not graded in the class, in part to give them a break from their academic **grind**, and so it was hard to tell whether their art appreciation was improving their diagnostic skills. But in **anonymous** journal entries from previous classes, the students—who take the course during their geriatric rotation, making home visits to elderly patients—seem to pay closer, and more **empathetic**, attention to their patients.

Partly intended to make better doctors by making better-rounded human beings, such art courses are being joined by other, mostly elective humanities courses—and in some medical schools, whole humanities departments—that bring playwrights, poets, actors, philosophers, and other imports from the liberal arts into the world of medicine.

Adapted from Kennedy, Randy. "At Some Medical Schools, Humanities Join the Curriculum." *New York Times* Apr. 2006 Print.

hand in hand: closely associated
wing: a section of a building connected to the main part
rotations: work shifts
underrated: underestimated in value or importance
strand: a single thin length
grind: excessively hard work
anonymous: written by people who would like their names to be kept secret
empathetic: understanding of people's feelings

Exercise 3 Understanding the text

Write *T* for true or *F* for false for each statement.

→ 17th century

_F_ 1. The study of art with medicine is a modern concept.

_F_ 2. Mount Sinai School of Medicine is the only medical school to offer courses in the humanities.

3 year ago

_F_ 3. According to Dr. Muller, medical schools haven't realized how essential it is to develop good observation skills.

_T_ 4. After viewing *The Proposal* briefly, students were able to describe the most intricate parts.

'; almost did great detail even the strand of thread.

_F_ 5. Dr. Muller didn't give grades to his students because he didn't think art-appreciation was a serious course.

Exercise 4 Responding to the text

Respond to the reading by answering the following questions.

1. What conclusions were made in the 2001 *Journal of the American Medical Association*?
   Looking at painting and sculpture can improve medical students obeprvational abilities.

2. How can the study of art lower the cost of health care? _____

   _____

   _____

3. According to Ms. Hirschwerk, what experience happens in an art museum that might be successfully transferred to a doctor/patient interaction? _____

   _____

   _____

4. What finally confirmed Dr. Muller's beliefs about the value of the art classes?

   _____

   _____

5. What are some of the other humanities courses that have become part of some medical school curricula? _____

   _____

   _____

Exercise 5 Freewriting

Write for ten to fifteen minutes in your journal. Choose from topics below or an idea of your own. Express your thoughts and feelings. Don't worry about mistakes.

- Choose any photograph, painting, or sculpture and describe it in as much detail as possible.
- Describe a memorable landmark or tourist attraction, such as the Eiffel Tower, the Taj Mahal, or the Great Pyramids.
- Compare two schools or universities in terms of their size, class enrollment, course offerings, tuition, and location.
- Write about two recent films you have seen. Compare the actors' performances, the films' themes, and the cinematography.
- Compare your hometown with another place you have visited. Describe both in terms of attractions, architecture, population, and natural environment.

In **Writing Process Step 2** you will . . .

- learn about comparison-contrast organization.
- brainstorm ideas and specific vocabulary to use in your writing.
- determine the audience and purpose for your comparison-contrast essay.
- learn to use search engines and to evaluate the reliability of sources.
- create an outline for your essay.

Writing Process Step 2 | Brainstorming and Outlining

WRITING TASK We often make comparisons in both our personal and academic lives. We may compare two of our favorite movies with a friend or discuss linguistic differences among various languages in a research seminar. In this unit, you will write an essay for a photography magazine. You will compare and contrast two photographs. You may choose the two photographs on page 36 or two photographs of your choice that share common features. Discuss how these photographs are alike or different. Organize your writing by using either block or point-by-point style. Go to the Web to use the Online Writing Tutor.

Exercise 1 Understanding your assignment

Read the Writing Task again, and respond to the statements and questions below. Then discuss your answers with a partner.

1. Underline the topic in the assignment. What will you write about?

   _____

   _____

2. Circle the publication. What publication are you being asked to write for?

   _____

   _____

3. List any words that tell you the rhetorical mode. _____

   _____

4. What two options does the assignment give for organizing your essay?

   _____

Critical Thinking Focus

Comparison and Contrast Signal Words
Sometimes an assignment will not directly state the rhetorical mode. You will have to determine the type of writing from the words in the assignment. These words are called **signal words.**

The following are signal words you might find in a comparison-contrast assignment.

Compare: similarities, both, comparable, alike, common, share, similar
Contrast: differences, dissimilar, diverge, unlike, unalike, differ, contrasting

Exercise 2 Identifying comparison and contrast signal words

Read the assignment below. Look for words of comparison and words of contrast. Fill in the graphic organizer with those words.

> Holidays are important for people in every country and from every culture. They help people remember and celebrate important events. They also give people a reason to gather with family and friends. Think of a holiday from your home country. How is it similar to a holiday in another country? What do the two events share in common? Conversely, how do the holidays differ? Write for someone who is not familiar with either holiday. Your essay should provide both what is alike and what is different about the historical background and the festivities of each holiday.

COMPARISON WORDS	CONTRAST WORDS
similar	

Exercise 3 Brainstorming Ideas

Look at the pictures you want to compare. Write three elements that you wish to compare in each photo. Write ideas for differences for each element under each photo. Write similarities in the final column.

POINTS OF COMPARISON	PHOTO 1	PHOTO 2	SIMILARITIES
Point 1			
Point 2			
Point 3			

A. Think about your audience. In this case they are readers of a photography magazine. How will they benefit from reading your essay? In the graphic organizer below, write notes about who you imagine will be reading your essay and about what message you want to give them.

AUDIENCE	PURPOSE

B. Answer the following questions about your audience and purpose.

1. Considering the audience, how formal will this essay need to be? _____

   _____

2. What will this audience already know about your topic? _____

   _____

3. What will your readers expect to learn from your essay? _____

   _____

Exercise 5 **Brainstorming vocabulary**

A. Select adjectives from the box, or use other adjectives to describe the mood of your two photographs. You may use an adjective more than once.

delicate	light	serious	nostalgic	mysterious	solemn
playful	active	carefree	gentle	soothing	competitive
fun	noble	lonely	friendly	refreshing	peaceful

Photo 1

refreshing fun mysterious
delicate

Photo 2

devout friendly soothing
peaceful nostalgic

B. Write three sentences that describe each photograph. Use adjectives from the lists you created on page 43. You may use more than one adjective in each sentence.

Photo 1

_____

_____

_____

_____

Photo 2

_____

_____

_____

_____

Research Focus

Using Search Engines

Before you begin a Web search, be clear about what you are looking for. Here are some questions you can ask.

- What is the goal of my research?

- Do I want the opinion of an expert or the general public?

- Do I need statistics and facts?

- What keywords can I use to find information related to my topic?

Evaluating Reliability of Websites

Trustworthy websites should be fair and accurate. It takes practice to evaluate websites, but there are some guidelines you can follow. Ask yourself:

- Who is the site's author and what credentials does he or she have? Avoid anonymous websites and sites that are clearly written by individuals without proper qualifications.

- Is the site from a reputable organization, such as a well-known museum, university, or news source?

- Is the writing academic and free of errors?

- How old is the information? Avoid websites that have not been updated regularly.

- What audience does the website address? Is it intended for professionals in the field or for the general public?

- Does the site provide information that is directly relevant to your research, or is it more appropriate for background information?

- Does the website provide evidence and information about its sources?

Exercise 6 Searching and analyzing websites

A. Find a photography or art review on the Internet, and complete the following chart.

QUESTIONS	FINDINGS
What keywords did you use?	
What website did you find?	
Who wrote the review?	
What are the author(s)' credentials?	
Is the writing style formal or informal?	
Is the viewpoint balanced or biased? How do you know?	
What is the date of the posting?	
Who is the intended audience?	

B. Using your findings, write a paragraph explaining why the website is or is not reliable. Discuss with a partner.

_____

_____

_____

_____

_____

Comparison-Contrast Organization

In a comparison-contrast essay, the writer identifies similarities and/or differences between two ideas or subjects that share common features or characteristics. There are two basic styles of organization for this type of essay; one is **block style,** and the other is **point-by-point style.**

When you compare two subjects, you will want to focus on several points of comparison. For example, when comparing the photographs of children on page 48, one writer chose to focus on the light, the children's expressions, and the movement shown in each photo.

The following graphic organizers show the differences between block and point-by-point styles for comparing the two photos.

Block Style Organization

In block style, each subject becomes the controlling idea of the paragraph, and the points of comparison become your details.

If you are comparing two photographs, body paragraph 1 would focus on the first photo, and body paragraph 2 would focus on the second photo. The points of comparison will be the same in both paragraphs.

Introduction
- The hook gives an interesting fact, quotation, or statistic to get the readers' attention.
- Background information gives information about each photograph such as the photographers' names and the titles of the photos. It may also provide information about the location where the photographs were taken.
- The thesis statement tells what is being compared. It also introduces the points of comparison.

Body Paragraph 1
- Subject 1: first photograph
- Point 1: light
- Point 2: expressions
- Point 3: movement

Photo 1 — Light, Expressions, Movement

Body Paragraph 2
- Subject 2: second photograph
- Point 1: light
- Point 2: expressions
- Point 3: movement

Photo 2 — Light, Expressions, Movement

Conclusion
- The conclusion emphasizes the strongest similarities or strongest differences between the two subjects.
- The conclusion may also provide an evaluation of the subjects.
- The conclusion may also provide an insight drawn from the comparison.

Point-by-Point Style Organization

In point-by-point style, the controlling idea for each body paragraph is one of the points of comparison. The subjects then provide the details. So, in this organizational style, you would compare the light in both photographs before moving on to a new paragraph.

Introduction

- The hook provides an interesting fact, quotation, or statistic to get the readers' attention.
- Background information gives information about each photograph such as the photographers' names and the titles of the photos. It may also provide information about the location where the photographs were taken.
- The thesis statement tells what is being compared. It also introduces the points of comparison.

Body Paragraph 1

- Point 1: light
- Subject 1: first photograph
- Subject 2: second photograph

```
        Light
       /     \
  Photo 1   Photo 2
```

Body Paragraph 2

- Point 2: expressions
- Subject 1: first photograph
- Subject 2: second photograph

```
      Expressions
       /     \
  Photo 1   Photo 2
```

Body Paragraph 3

- Point 3: movement
- Subject 1: first photograph
- Subject 2: second photograph

```
       Movement
       /     \
  Photo 1   Photo 2
```

Conclusion

- The conclusion emphasizes the strongest similarities or differences between the two subjects.
- The conclusion may also provide an evaluation of the subjects.
- Sometimes the conclusion will provide an insight that the writer has drawn from the comparison.

Exercise 7 Reading a student essay

Look at the images. Then read the essay below. How does the writer interpret the emotions of the children?

Village School by Margaret Bourke-White

Children's Puppet Theatre, Paris 1963 by Alfred Eisenstaedt

Capturing Children's Emotions

Looking at children in different settings, one can see the honesty in their expressions. They may be happy or sad, playful or serious, but there is always integrity in their emotions. Children are the focus of two photographs: *Village School* by Margaret Bourke-White and *Children's Puppet Theatre, Paris 1963* by Alfred Eisenstaedt. In both photographs, children are staring at something, but the light, expressions, and body language differ greatly across the two photographs.

In the Bourke-White photograph, rows of young boys are confined in a dark classroom. The dark light creates a serious mood. Even the sides of the picture are dark. The only light in the room shines on the faces and heads of the boys. This suggests that the photographer wanted to emphasize the children's intellects while the children's emotions are suppressed. Even though there is something frightening about this photograph, all the boys have dignity and appear to have strong individual personalities. The school may be strict, but the children are not defeated. The boys sit up straight on uncomfortable-looking wooden benches with their arms out of view. They sit in four rows with faces staring straight ahead. There are large gaps between them. None of the boys touches another, and there appears to be no movement or communication. This arrangement creates a feeling of isolation. However, the boy in front whose face is the largest and whose body you cannot see at all, has a look of hope.

In stark contrast to *Village School*, the children in *Children's Puppet Theatre* are outdoors and having a good time. The photograph is light. Although there is no color, the textures of the woolen sweaters give the photograph a warm feel. The expressions on the children's faces vary greatly. Some laugh out loud, while others hold their hands over their faces. A few are shouting, and some are in awe. One boy covers his ears, which suggests loud sounds. In fact, the whole feeling is loud, bright, and fun. The children are able to release their emotions and show exactly how they feel. There is no inhibition. In contrast to the school boys, these children are not in neat rows, but seem to be in motion, touching, leaning, and hugging. They display their personalities openly, not quietly as in *Village School*. The children in the Eisenstaedt photograph, both boys and girls, are all bunched together. The main center of interest is a little boy whose mouth is wide open and whose right hand shoots out in front of him.

Two groups of children are depicted in these two photographs. One conveys the strength and stillness of the boys. One is structured and the other is free. One shows contrast through light and dark. It focuses on the children's faces. The other also focuses on the children's faces, but it does so by capturing many extreme and diverse expressions. The two photographs show movement versus stillness. The personalities and individuality of the children draw viewers into both photographs in dramatic ways.

Exercise 8 Examining the student essay

A. Respond to the essay by answering the following questions.

1. What is the difference in how the children are positioned in the two photographs?

   orderly row — serious, surpless , no order — active

2. How does light contribute to the moods of each photograph?

   Dark — serious   light — warm

3. Why are the expressions on the children's faces in both photographs so important?

   Their face can exparess their emotion

B. Examine the organization of the essay by responding to the questions and statements below. Then compare your answers with a partner.

1. Circle the hook.
2. Underline the thesis statement.
3. What elements are used to compare and contrast the two subjects?

   light , expressions , body language

4. Which organizational style does the writer use?

   _____ point-by-point   ✓ block

5. What similarities and differences are restated in the conclusion? _____

   stillness — free , light — dark.

Exercise 9 Writing an outline

GO ONLINE

Review your brainstorming ideas and your freewriting exercise. Then go to the Web to print out an outline template for your essay.

In **Writing Process Step 3** you will . . .

- learn about prepositional phrases.
- write a first draft of your comparison-contrast essay.

Exercise 1 Reading a student essay

Refer back to the photographs on page 48. How does this writer respond to the children's faces?

The Expressions of Youth

Seeing the emotions expressed in children's faces can elicit powerful responses from the viewer. Children laughing outrageously can brighten up a person's day. Thoughtful, solemn, or introverted feelings can touch people deeply as well. The photographs, Margaret Bourke-White's *Village School* and Alfred Eisenstaedt's *Children's Puppet Theatre, Paris 1963* both have children as the central figures. *Village School* shows the more serious side, whereas *Children's Puppet Theatre* reveals the freedom of youth. Although both photographs display a transparency of feeling, the light, the facial expressions of the subjects, body language, and spatial positioning are different.

Light is one of the most important elements of any photograph. It can set the tone, establish the mood, and create the focus of the picture. In *Village School* the periphery and the room are dark and barren, with nothing to brighten them up. This gives the photograph a heavy feeling. The light shining on the faces and heads of the boys draws the viewer in with its almost ghostlike quality, contrasting sharply with their somber clothing. The light shining on the boy in the first row singles him out, giving a feeling of isolation. Conversely, the light in *Children's Puppet Theatre* spreads equally across the photo, exposing the different shades and textures of clothing from black to gray to white. It seems as if the entire photograph is bursting with light, creating a cheerful mood, unlike the mysterious mood of *Village School*.

Facial expressions can reveal joy, pain, suffering, dignity, and humanity in a good photograph. The young boys in *Village School* appear concerned or even worried. Perhaps the person who is in charge is very strict and severe.

As a consequence, the children remain quiet and controlled. The serious expressions on their faces suggest that they understand what is required of them. On the other hand, in *Children's Puppet Theatre*, a crowd of excited children, both boys and girls, have been caught in a vivid moment of spontaneous joy. Their expressions are so real that viewers can almost imagine the puppets they are watching. Some children are shouting with mouths wide open. Others look astonished, eyes almost bulging out with lips curled or tightly shut.

Spatial relationships and the body language that subjects use unlock the story of a photograph. The boys in *Village School* all sit, one behind the other, on benches. They sit up straight, separated from each other, and facing forward. This rigid atmosphere suggests that communication between the boys is very limited. In contrast, with their bodies pressed closely together, the children in *Children's Puppet Theatre* are free to express whatever they are feeling. One child spontaneously raises his arm pointing toward the stage. In front, another boy covers his ears. Maybe the sound is too loud or he does not like what he hears. The two girls at the bottom right look on, leaning against each other with one girl resting her head on the other's shoulder. There is a sense of trust and support as the young children enthusiastically respond to the thrilling performance before them.

Photographs have an amazing power to transmit energy visually. Both of these photographs depict children who are looking at someone or something that the viewer cannot see. However, diverse moods expressed through lighting, facial expressions, positioning, and body language emerge from each image. These photos captivate the viewer not by what the children are watching but by how they react. The children's emotions draw viewers into their reality.

Exercise 2 **Examining the student essay**

A. Respond to the essay by answering the following questions.

1. How are the ideas in this essay similar to those in the essay on pages 48–49?

   They describe the same points but in different way.

2. How are the examples and details in this essay different from the one on pages 48–49?

   The previous article use block while this article use point by point.

B. Examine the organization of the essay by responding to the question and statement below.

1. Underline the thesis statement.
2. What organizational style does this writer use in this essay?

   point by point

Language and Grammar Focus

Prepositions and Prepositional Phrases

Prepositions are words such as *at, in, on,* and *next to.* A preposition can be used in a phrase with a noun or pronoun to show relationships between people and objects—this is called a *prepositional phrase.* **Prepositional phrases** can also be used to show location and spatial order.

The children are sitting **on wooden benches.**

Prepositional Phrases Showing Spatial Relationships

Prepositions like *by, for, of, to, with,* and *on* can be used in prepositional phrases to show spatial relationships between people and objects.

The boy is standing **to the right of his mother.**

Prepositional Phrases Showing Location

Prepositional phrases can also be used in descriptions to show location.

There is an old house **in the background.**

Prepositions

above	below	beneath	over	in front of	next to

Prepositional Phrases

in the background	on the left	on the right
in the center	on the periphery	on the sides
in the foreground		

Exercise 3 Identifying prepositions

Choose the correct preposition from the box to complete the sentences.

by	for	of	to	in	on

1. The little girl is resting her head _____on_____ her mother's shoulder.

2. The three children are posing _____ the camera.

3. The two women were having lunch _____ the pool.

4. On the left side _____ the photograph are two large trees.

5. The woman _____ the flowered hat is sitting in the front row.

6. The little boy was waving goodbye _____ his grandmother.

Exercise 4 Using prepositional phrases in sentences

Write sentences about the photographs on page 36. Use a prepositional phrase from the Language and Grammar Focus on page 53 in each sentence.

1. the ocean _____

_____

2. the young girl _____

_____

3. the kite _____

_____

4. the father and son _____

_____

5. the bicycle _____

_____

Exercise 5 Writing a first draft

GO ONLINE

Review your outline. Then write your first draft of a comparison-contrast essay in response to your two photographs. Go to the Web to use the Online Writing Tutor.

Exercise 6 Peer editing a first draft

GO ONLINE

A. After writing a first draft, it is helpful to get feedback on your ideas. Exchange essays with two other people. For each essay you read, answer the Peer Editor's Questions on a separate piece of paper. Discuss your responses.

Peer Editor's Questions

1. What is your favorite part of the essay?

2. What elements of comparison is the writer using to compare the photos?

3. What organizational style did the writer use?

4. What parts of the essay could be supported with more detail?

5. What one suggestion would you make to the writer to improve the essay?

Go to the Web to print out a peer editor's worksheet.

B. Review your feedback and the organization guidelines on pages 46–47. Make notes for your revision. In this step, you may add, remove, or rewrite information to clarify your ideas.

 In **Writing Process Step 4** you will . . .

• learn about restrictive and nonrestrictive relative clauses.
• edit your first draft and write a final draft.

Now that you have written a first draft, it is time to edit. Editing involves making changes to your writing to improve it and to correct mistakes.

Language and Grammar Focus

Relative Clauses

Relative clauses (also called adjective clauses) modify nouns or noun phrases. They are dependent clauses and must be attached to a main clause.

• A relative clause must always follow the noun to which it refers.

His favorite author wrote the <u>book</u> which he left on the airplane.

• There are two types of relative clauses: **restrictive** and **nonrestrictive.**

Restrictive Relative Clauses

A restrictive relative clause gives essential information that helps identify or define the noun or noun phrase it modifies.

That is the <u>woman</u> **who sits next to me in French class.**

In restrictive clauses, use the relative pronouns *who* or *that* for people, and *which* or *that* for things and animals.

My father is the man **who** is wearing a green tie.

We will pick you up in a black car **that** has red flames along the sides.

Do not use a comma between the noun and the relative pronoun.

Nonrestrictive Relative Clauses

A nonrestrictive relative clause gives extra information about a noun or noun phrase.

<u>Walker Evans</u>, **who collaborated with the writer James Agee,** was a famous 20th-century photographer.

In nonrestrictive relative clauses, use *who* for people and *which* for things.

The photograph, **which** was taken on a bleak day in La Paz, won a prize at the state fair.

Use commas to separate the clause from the rest of the sentence.

Rhein II, which is a simple-looking photograph of the Rhine River, sold for more than four million dollars in an auction.

 Do not use the word *that* in a nonrestrictive relative clause.

RESTRICTIVE RELATIVE CLAUSES AFTER THE MAIN CLAUSE

MAIN CLAUSE		RELATIVE CLAUSE		
	NOUN	SUBJECT RELATIVE PRONOUN	VERB	
I know	a photographer	**who** **that**	**travels**	all over the world.
They take	photographs	**which** **that**	**appear**	in museums.

RESTRICTIVE RELATIVE CLAUSES INSIDE THE MAIN CLAUSE

MAIN CLAUSE				
NOUN	SUBJECT RELATIVE PRONOUN	VERB		
The photographer	**who** **that**	**travels**	all over the world	won't use a digital camera.
The photographs	**which** **that**	**appear**	in museums	are extremely famous.

NONRESTRICTIVE RELATIVE CLAUSES AFTER THE MAIN CLAUSE

MAIN CLAUSE		RELATIVE CLAUSE		
	NOUN	SUBJECT RELATIVE PRONOUN	VERB	
I know	Sam,	**who**	**travels**	all over the world.
Everyone likes	the photographs,	**which**	**are**	extremely expensive.

NONRESTRICTIVE RELATIVE CLAUSES INSIDE THE MAIN CLAUSE

MAIN CLAUSE	RELATIVE CLAUSE			
NOUN	SUBJECT RELATIVE PRONOUN	VERB		
Sam,	**who**	**travels**	all over the world,	won't use a digital camera.
Bravo's photographs,	**which**	**are**	extremely expensive,	appear in museums.

Exercise 1 Identifying restrictive and nonrestrictive clauses

Underline the relative clauses. If the sentence is a restrictive relative clause, write *R*. If the sentence is a nonrestrictive clause, write *NR*.

_R_ 1. The photographer who was also a set designer was Cecil Beaton.

_____ 2. Henri Cartier-Bresson, who was a very famous photojournalist, took photographs of real-life situations.

_____ 3. The photographs that were taken by Lewis Hine depict children working in factories.

_____ 4. Many of the photographs that were taken by Manuel Álvarez Bravo were of inanimate objects.

Exercise 2 Combining sentences using restrictive relative clauses

Use a restrictive relative clause to combine each pair of sentences.

1. Photographs are taken indoors. They often require special lighting.

   Photographs that are taken indoors often require special lighting.

   _____

2. Photographers should not take pictures in the direction of the sun. They are photographing outdoors.

   _____

   _____

3. Ansel Adams took photographs. They portrayed beautiful scenes in nature.

   _____

   _____

4. Photographs can be transferred from one document to another. They are digital.

   _____

   _____

5. Telephoto lenses are good for photographing wildlife. They often make objects appear closer.

   _____

   _____

6. Photographs cannot be manipulated easily. They are taken with film.

   _____

   _____

Exercise 3 Combining sentences using nonrestrictive relative clauses

Use a nonrestrictive relative clause to combine each pair of sentences.

1. Photojournalism focuses on newsworthy events. It is one career path for photographers.

   Photojournalism, which is one career path for photographers, focuses on newsworthy events.

2. The Japanese created anime. They have contributed to the film industry.

   _____

   _____

3. The digital camera is used worldwide. It allows people to send photos over the Internet.

   _____

   _____

   _____

4. Louis Daguerre was a French inventor. He developed the diorama.

   _____

   _____

GO ONLINE

Language and Grammar Focus

Relative Clauses with *Whose*

Whose is the **relative pronoun** that shows possession. It takes the place of the pronouns *his, her, its, their,* or the possessive form of the noun. It is always followed by a noun.

Whose is used for both people and things.

   Adolfo, **whose** parents live in Mexico, likes to go hiking in Utah.

   The camera **whose** case is leather belongs to my husband.

Whose can be used with both restrictive and nonrestrictive clauses.

   The girl **whose hair is in rollers** is getting her hair straightened.

   Maria, **whose father owns that factory**, is one of our clients.

Exercise 4 Combining sentences with *whose*

Use a restrictive or nonrestrictive relative clause with *whose* to combine each pair of sentences.

1. The boy is standing by the tree. His overalls are torn.

   The boy whose overalls are torn is standing by the tree.

   _____

2. There are many photographs in the book. Their sizes have been changed.

   _____

   _____

3. Richard Avedon was a world-renowned portrait photographer. His pictures were of famous celebrities.

   _____

   _____

   _____

4. Yousuf Karsh was born in Armenia. His photograph of Winston Churchill brought him international fame.

   _____

   _____

   _____

5. Galleries attract large crowds. Their exhibits are often controversial.

   _____

   _____

6. Katsushika Hokusai lived in the 19th century. His painting is one of Japan's most famous.

   _____

   _____

   _____

7. Frida Kahlo was injured as a young adult. Her paintings were often self-portraits.

   _____

   _____

Exercise 5 Editing a paragraph

Read the paragraph, and edit as necessary. There are four more mistakes in restrictive and nonrestrictive relative clauses.

For anyone thinking of photography as a career, there are many exciting alternatives. For those ~~who~~ *whose* ambition is to be where the action is and who are not afraid of taking risks, photojournalism provides many thrilling possibilities. However, you may find yourself in a forest fire that could be life-threatening. Do you like to work in the outdoors? Then wildlife photography is a job who captures animals in their natural habitats. If creating posters, magazine layouts, and brochures in a large corporation sounds interesting to you, there is advertising photography. Law-enforcement photographers shoot crime scenes, who help police solve important cases. Sports photographers, their job is to freeze one perfect moment in time, often need to take hundreds of photos in quick succession to get the desired shot. Fashion photography, who may seem glamorous to some people, is really focused on selling clothing and can be very competitive. Do you ever wonder how restaurant menus can make the French fries look better in the picture than on your plate? Then you might want to take pictures of food. However, taking pictures is not as easy as baking bread. Taking a photograph is like painting a picture. It requires skill, creativity, and an eye for detail.

Exercise 6 Editing your first draft and rewriting

Review your essay for content, organization, and language mistakes. Use the checklist below. Then write a final draft. Go to the Web to use the Online Writing Tutor.

GO ONLINE

Editor's Checklist

Put a check (✓) as appropriate.

CONTENT AND ORGANIZATION

○ 1. Does your introduction tell enough about what photos you will compare and what points you will use to compare them?

○ 2. Did you use block or point-by-point organization correctly?

○ 3. Does the conclusion evaluate the effects of the photographs on the viewer?

LANGUAGE

○ 4. Did you use prepositions correctly when describing the placement of objects and people in each photo?

○ 5. Did you use restrictive and nonrestrictive clauses correctly?

○ 6. Did you use *whose* for possession with people and things? If yes, is *whose* followed by a noun or noun phrase?

Go to the Web to print out a peer editor's worksheet.

 In **Review** you will . . .

- practice identifying prepositions.
- practice using restrictive and nonrestrictive relative clauses.

In Putting It All Together, you will review the concepts you learned in this unit.

Exercise 1 Identifying prepositions

Choose the correct preposition from the box to complete the sentences.

by	for	of	in	with	on

1. Three tired children are reclining _____ the sofa.

2. The smiling newspaper boy is standing _____ the fence.

3. The filmmakers organized a benefit _____ disabled children.

4. The man _____ the pipe is sitting next to his wife.

5. The street musicians were playing in front _____ the subway station.

6. The woman _____ the pink dress looks sad.

Exercise 2 Combining sentences using restrictive relative clauses

Use a restrictive relative clause to combine each pair of sentences.

1. The cinematographer is George Lucas. He is best known for special effects.

   _____

   _____

   _____

2. I broke my camera lense. It was for my new camera.

   _____

   _____

3. The camera case was stolen. It was bought in Italy.

   _____

   _____

4. Petra was crowded with people. They were all taking pictures at the same time.

_____

_____

5. Reporters invade people's privacy. They take pictures of celebrities.

_____

_____

Exercise 3 Combining sentences using nonrestrictive relative clauses

Use a nonrestrictive relative clause to combine each pair of sentences.

1. Nobuyoshi Araki was born in Tokyo. He is one of the most famous modern Japanese photographers.

_____

_____

2. The camera obscura was a primitive type of camera. It was made from a box with a small pinhole opening.

_____

_____

3. Alfred Stieglitz worked hard to make people accept photography as an art form. He was married to the famous painter Georgia O'Keeffe.

_____

_____

_____

4. The Polaroid camera produced instant photographs. It was invented by Edwin Land in 1946.

_____

_____

5. The first practical process of photography was invented by Daguerre. He was born in 1787.

_____

_____

Exercise 4 **Combining sentences with *whose***

Use a restrictive or nonrestrictive relative clause with *whose* to combine each pair of sentences.

1. The man filed a police report. His camera was stolen.

   _____

   _____

2. The woman lives in Istanbul. Her bag was lost.

   _____

   _____

3. The local 24-hour photo shop has a booming business. Its promotional advertisements entice lots of customers.

   _____

   _____

4. The $500 prize went to the young photographer. Her subject matter was her cat.

   _____

   _____

5. The students were advised to reapply in the spring. Their applications were turned down.

   _____

   _____

6. Quang-Tuan Luong has visited all the national parks in the United States. His photographs have been shown on television.

   _____

   _____

7. The woman lives in a small village. Her artwork sells for high prices.

   _____

   _____

Exercise 5 Editing a paragraph

Read the paragraph, and edit as necessary. There are seven mistakes, including two mistakes in punctuation.

The camera, was invented in 1837, has had many different professional and personal uses. One of the earliest professional photographers was Julia Cameron, who objective was to make photographs the way a painter would create a painting. These photographs looked like the portraits, that were painted then. Mathew Brady, who was the greatest photojournalist of the Civil War period informed the public about the realities of war. Photojournalism was also used to depict life during the Great Depression. For example, photographers like Dorothea Lange took emotional photos of the dust storms in Oklahoma, whose displaced families from their homes. Photos have become a necessity for families they want to chronicle the milestones in their children's lives. Photos, are an essential part of any wedding, are cherished by families around the world.

 In **Timed Writing** you will . . .

- practice writing with a time limit.

Write a comparison-contrast essay in response to these two photographs. Before you begin, review the suggested time management strategy below.

Women Jumping Rope During Eid

Soccer 2005—East Asian Football Championship—North Korea vs. Japan

Step 1 **BRAINSTORMING:** 5 minutes

Write down ideas and vocabulary for your essay. Use the chart below.

POINTS OF COMPARISON	PHOTO 1	PHOTO 2	SIMILARITIES
Point 1			
Point 2			
Point 3			

Test-Taking Tip

Leave wide margins as you write so that you can make changes easily when you edit your essay.

OUTLINING: 5 minutes

Write an outline for your essay.

Introduction (First Paragraph)	
Hook Capture the reader's attention by focusing on a unique aspect of the subject.	
Background Information Provide information about each photograph such as the name of the photo.	
Thesis Statement Tell what points will be compared.	
Body Paragraphs (Middle Paragraphs)	
Block Style Discuss the first photo using the points of comparison. **Point-by-Point Style** Discuss the first point of comparison and how it relates to each photo.	
Block Style Discuss the second photo using the points of comparison. **Point-by-Point Style** Discuss both photos against the second point of comparison.	
Conclusion (Last Paragraph)	
Summary Emphasize the strongest similarities or contrasts between the two subjects.	

WRITING: 40 minutes

Use your brainstorming notes and outline to write your essay on a separate piece of paper.

EDITING: 10 minutes

When you have finished your essay, check it for mistakes. Use this checklist.

GO ONLINE

Editor's Checklist

Put a check (✓) as appropriate.

○ 1. Does the introduction provide background information?

○ 2. Did you include an analysis of each point of comparison for each body paragraph?

○ 3. Did you explain the similarities and differences between the photographs?

○ 4. Did you use restrictive and nonrestrictive relative clauses correctly?

○ 5. Did you use *whose* to show possession in restrictive or nonrestrictive clauses? If yes, is *whose* followed by a noun?

○ 6. Did you use prepositional phrases to describe the placement of people and items in each photo?

Go to the Web to print out a peer editor's worksheet.

Test-Taking Tip

Read your essay one last time to see how you can improve it for a higher score.

Topics for Future Writing

Write a comparison-contrast essay on one of the following topics.

Dietary Health: Nutritionists often study differences in the way people eat. Compare your diet with that of a person in another country. Is one healthier than the other? Why?

Graphic Design: There are many different graphic design programs on the market. Compare two different software programs. What are the benefits of each? What are the drawbacks? Would you recommend one over the other?

History: Something in the human spirit calls us to explore the world around us. We generally consider the 15th to 17th centuries to have been the Age of Exploration. Yet, a new spurt of exploration developed in the 20th and 21st centuries with the Space Age. What similarities and differences can be drawn between the two ages?

Literature: Compare two novelists and their work. Explore the authors' characters, themes, or styles. What makes each novelist memorable?

Marketing: Compare and contrast two marketing campaigns. In what ways does each draw people to the products? Which campaign is more effective? Why?

Psychology: Explain how physical beauty differs from inner beauty.

Sociology: There are many reasons people choose where to live. Some people prefer living in cities. Others prefer living outside of cities. Compare urban and suburban lifestyles. Which lifestyle is healthier? Which is the most attractive option for you? Why?

UNIT 3
Cause-and-Effect Essays

Unit Goals

Critical Thinking Focus

- cause-and-effect signal words

Research Focus

- quoting from a source

Rhetorical Focus

- cause-and-effect organization
- relating effects to causes

Language and Grammar Focus

- collocations with cause-and-effect signal words
- sentence connectors showing cause and effect
- real and unreal conditionals

To find answers in life people read books, conduct research, ask questions, and seek information from experts. Analyzing causes and effects helps people answer questions about why things happen. In this unit, you will explore the causes and effects of different physical, psychological, and emotional conditions.

Exercise 1 Thinking about the topic

A. Discuss the cartoon with a partner.

- What is the message of the cartoon? there is a maze in the cartoon.
- Why is it difficult to find happiness in life? People have to try many times to the destionation,
- What suggestion would you give to someone who is looking for happiness?

Broke the rules just like broke the wall in the maze, go directly to the goal,

B. Make notes about what has brought you happiness in your life. Then discuss in small groups.

watching soccer game,
hang out with friends
play video game
when I see my stocks rise
chat with my family and friends
play soccer
get good grades

In his search for what makes people happy, filmmaker Aaron Mighty created a documentary called *One Happy Movie*. What did he discover?

What Makes People Happy?
Young Filmmaker Finds the Answer

While his childhood friends stayed in Harlem in New York City, Aaron Mighty went to college. As his college **peers** spent their money on fraternities and parties, Mighty invested in the stock market. When his graduate school colleagues **sought out** teachers to ask questions, Mighty spent nearly $10,000 to get an answer.

Plagued with self-doubt and uncertainty about his future, he wondered, "What makes people happy?" He found the answer in making the feature documentary film *One Happy Movie.* The film **catalogs** a cross-country road trip by four college students visiting a variety of cities, towns, and landmarks, **posing** the question to a large number of people.

"The originality of the concept is what intrigued people," Mighty said. "When I first told people I was making a film about happiness, they **mocked** me and said, 'There's no happiness in the world,' but obviously there is. A lot of people, especially college-age people, think about it all the time. We constantly think about our direction, what our focus is, and what we want to do in life to make us happy."

The director of the project, David Acevedo, agrees and said he was **drawn to** directing the project because he wanted to see how answers would change depending on people's social, economic, and racial background.

"We got several deep responses and many **weird** responses about what made people happy," Acevedo said. "It surprised me how people could be from so many different social or racial backgrounds, people of all ages, from small towns to big cities, rich and poor, young and old, but so many of them had such similar answers."

The young filmmaker feels satisfied that he learned the answer to the question he set off to answer years ago, regardless of how much money the film generates.

"I know now what the answer is," Mighty said. "It is the simple things in life. It's not about what kind of car you drive, how much money you make, how big your house is. Those are things that are truly **irrelevant,** and those are things in the most part we didn't get from people. I've learned that life is just about living. It's about going out there and enjoying life and being happy."

Adapted from Xavier, Patricia. "What Makes People Happy: Young Filmmaker Finds the Answer." *Young Money.* Interchange Education Foundation, Inc. 11 Mar. 2004. Web. 30 May 2012.

peers: people of the same age or class
sought out: looked for
plagued: overwhelmed
catalogs: describes
posing: asking

mocked: made fun of
drawn to: interested in
weird: strange; unusual
irrelevant: having nothing to do with the subject

Exercise 3 Understanding the text

Write *T* for true or *F* for false for each statement.

_F_ 1. For his documentary, Aaron Mighty interviewed students from his college.

_F_ 2. He was confident about his future.

_F_ 3. People thought that the idea for his movie was original.

_T_ 4. He was not concerned about how much money the movie would earn.

_T/F_ 5. According to Mighty, a beautiful home, money, and a nice car will not bring happiness.

Exercise 4 Responding to the text

Respond to the reading by answering the following questions. Then discuss your answers with a partner.

1. What made Mighty different from his peers?

   His friends spend money on fratomities or parties, while he spend money on ivest on stock market.

2. How did Mighty find answers to his questions?

   He found answers during making a film.

3. What were Mighty's conclusions about happiness?

It is simple things in life.

4. In your opinion, what are some of the simple things in life?

Shine my belt, success in knob year.

Freewriting

Write for ten to fifteen minutes in your journal. Choose from the topics below or an idea of your own. Express your thoughts and feelings. Don't worry about mistakes.

- Aaron Mighty says, "I've learned that life is just about living. It's about going out there and enjoying life and being happy." What do you think this means? Do you agree or disagree with him?
- What goals do you have in life that you think will bring you fulfillment? How can you achieve these goals?
- Write about an experience in your life that made you feel happy, sad, angry, or frustrated.
- How does appearance affect the way a person is perceived by others?
- How does criticism affect people emotionally?

In **Writing Process Step 2** you will . . .

- learn how to analyze a cause-and-effect assignment.
- learn about cause-and-effect organization.
- brainstorm ideas and specific vocabulary to use in your writing.
- determine the audience and purpose for your cause-and-effect essay.
- learn how to quote outside sources.
- create an outline for a cause-and-effect essay.

WRITING TASK In life we are often concerned with how and why physical, emotional, or psychological conditions or behaviors affect us. What makes people happy? How do people act when they are frustrated? What are the motives of betrayal? What are the results of being betrayed? In this unit you will write an essay for a popular health magazine. Explore the multiple causes or effects of an emotional, psychological, or physical condition. Discuss reasons, consequences, and/or outcomes. Include at least one quotation from a reliable outside source. Go to the Web to use the Online Writing Tutor.

Exercise 1 Understanding your assignment

Read the writing task again, and respond to the questions and statements below. Discuss your answers with a partner.

1. Underline the topic you are asked to write about.

2. List some emotions or conditions that interest you. _____

_____

3. What publication are you being asked to write for? _____

_____

4. What should you include in your essay? _____

_____

Critical Thinking Focus

Cause-and-Effect Signal Words
The following are signal words you might find in a cause-and-effect assignment.

affect *v.* to have an effect on; to make a difference to

consequence *n.* a result or effect of an action or condition

grounds *n.* factors forming a basis for action or the justification for a belief

impact *v.* or *n.* have a strong effect on someone or something

implication *n.* a likely consequence of something

intention *n.* a thing intended; an aim or plan

motive *n.* a reason for doing something

outcome *n.* the way a thing turns out; a consequence

promote *v.* to further the progress of (something)

reason *n.* a cause, explanation, or justification for an action or event

result *n.* a consequence, effect, or outcome of something

Exercise 2 Identifying signal words for cause or effect

Decide which of the words below relate to causes and which relate to effects. Then write them in the appropriate column.

| affect | consequence | grounds | impact | implication | intention |
| motive | outcome | reason | result | promote | |

CAUSES	EFFECTS
affect	result
motive	impact
intention	outcome
promote	consequence
reason	implication
grounds	

Language and Grammar Focus

Collocations with Cause-and-Effect Signal Words

Some signal words in cause-and-effect assignments and essays are regularly followed by specific prepositions. The signal word and the preposition travel together to convey the desired meaning.

NOUNS	PREPOSITIONS	EXAMPLES
outcome	of	A positive outlook can change the **outcomes of** your life.
impact	on	Discuss the story's **impact on** your readers.
reason	for	There are many **reasons for** laughing and thinking positively.
grounds	for	You have many **grounds for** being angry.

VERBS	PREPOSITIONS	EXAMPLES
lead	to	Recognizing what makes you happy can **lead to** a more productive life.
result	in	A wrong decision may **result in** a waste of time and money.

Exercise 3 | Using cause-and-effect signal words and collocations

Use the signal words and prepositions to write sentences about a physical, emotional, or psychological condition you might write about for your essay.

1. Long time spend on electrical device outcome of sight damaging.

2. Social media may lead to high wave of emotion.

3. Internet addition results in anxiety problem due to instant information.   long-term
                                                                                  unabl

Exercise 4 | Brainstorming ideas

Choose an emotion or condition that you would like to write about. Write it in the middle of the chart. On the left, note three different causes of that condition. On the right, list three effects.

CAUSES	CONDITION	EFFECTS

If you find the causes more interesting, focus on the causes in your essay.
If you find the effects more interesting, your focus should be on the effects.

Exercise 5 | Considering audience and purpose

A. Think about your audience. In this case, they are readers of a popular health magazine. How will they benefit from reading your essay? In the graphic organizer below, write notes about who you imagine will be reading your essay and about what message you want to give them.

AUDIENCE	PURPOSE

B. Answer the following questions about your audience and purpose.

1. Considering the audience, how formal will this essay need to be? _____

   _____

2. What will this audience already know about your topic? _____

   _____

3. What will your readers expect to learn from your essay? _____

   _____

Exercise 6 Brainstorming vocabulary

On a separate piece of paper, create a word web like the one below. Fill it in with words related to your topic. Use a dictionary or thesaurus to find more words you might need. The example here shows words a student used to write about happiness.

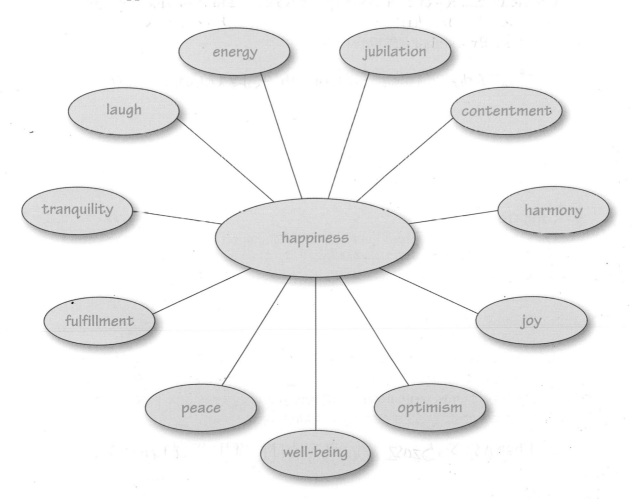

Quoting from a Source

In academic essays writers often quote other sources for emphasis, explanation, and credibility. When using a direct quotation follow these basic rules.

• Copy the text exactly as it appears.

• For short quotations, use quotation marks at the beginning and end of the quotation.

• For quotations of four lines or more, indent the quotation one inch from the left margin to set it off from the rest of the text.

• Be sure to give credit to your source by telling your readers where your quotation is from.

Short Quotations

Use the following punctuation and capitalization for short quotations.

• Begin the quotation with a capital letter if it is a complete sentence.

• Separate the quotation from the sentence with a comma.

• Place the final punctuation inside the quotation marks.

> Malcolm Gladwell says in his popular book *Outliers*, "Working really hard is what successful people do."

> "Working really hard is what successful people do," says Malcolm Gladwell in his popular book *Outliers*.

Short Quotations Separated by Text

When you divide a quotation, use the following rules.

• Enclose both parts with quotation marks.

• Use a lowercase letter to begin the second part.

• Place commas after the first part of the quotation and before the second part.

> "If you work hard and assert yourself and use your mind and imagination," according to Gladwell, "you can shape the world to your desires."

Long Quotations

Quotations longer than four lines do not use quotation marks. Follow these rules for longer quotations.

• Indent one inch from the left margin.

• Place one line below the main text.

> In her article "How Attitude Affects Your Health," Dr. Deyanira Wong explains:

>> The body releases stress hormones when people have negative attitudes. These hormones may cause temporary health problems such as headaches, upset stomach, or back pain. With long term stress and negativity, people may suffer from increased blood pressure, blood clots, insomnia, and chest pain associated with cardiovascular and heart disease. Attitudes may also have an effect on the body's immune system.

Research Focus

Common Verbs and Phrases Used to Introduce Quotations

Some common verbs and phrases that can be used to introduce quotations are: *mention, claim, say, state, suggest, continue, believe, advise, explain,* and *according to.* These verbs and phrases connect the quotation with the attribution. The attribution, or the source, can be a person or an institution.

| attribution | | quotation |

American author Mark Twain advised, "to get the full value of joy, you must have somebody to divide it with."

Exercise 7 Using correct punctuation with quotations

Read the following quotations and attributions. Add proper punctuation to identify the quotation and the attribution.

1. Mohandas Gandhi believed "Happiness is when what you think, what you say, and what you do are in harmony."

2. "Be careful what you water your dreams with" suggests the Chinese philosopher Lao Tzu, "Water them with worry and fear and you will produce weeds that choke the life from your dream. Water them with optimism and solutions and you will cultivate success."

3. On the topic of acquiring knowledge, Doris Lessing explains "That is what learning is. You suddenly understand something you've understood all your life, but in a new way."

4. "Research is to see what everybody else has seen" claims the Nobel Prize winner Albert Szent-Györgyi "and to think what nobody else has thought."

5. According to Maxim Gorky "happiness always looks small while you hold it in your hands, but let it go, and you learn at once how big and precious it is."

6. "We tend to forget that happiness doesn't come as a result of getting something we don't have" Fredrick Koeing states "but rather of recognizing and appreciating what we do have."

7. The Persian poet Hafiz once said "ever since happiness heard your name, it has been running through the streets trying to find you."

Exercise 8 Attributing quotations to their sources

Refer to the chart below to write sentences introducing each quotation and attributing the quotation to the author. The first item is done for you.

Attribution

QUOTATION	AUTHOR(S)	VERB/ PHRASE
Among the Ibo the art of conversation is regarded very highly, and proverbs are the palm-oil with which words are eaten.	Chinua Achebe	states
Feeling happy generally goes along with feeling confident, optimistic, and energetic, all great traits for finding success.	Tina Adler	says
The verdict is in: Wealth does not make us happy.	Phil Brown	according to
The secret is here in the present. If you pay attention to the present, you can improve upon it.	Paulo Coehlo	suggests
The self is not something one finds, it is something one creates.	Thomas S. Szasz	claims

1. "Among the Ibo," Achebe states, "the art of conversation is regarded very highly, and proverbs are the palm-oil with which words are eaten."

2. Tina Adler says, "Feeling "" for finding success."

3. "The verdict "" happy.", according to Phil Brown.

4. Paulo Coehlo suggests, "The secret "" it."

5. Thomas S. Szasz claims, "The self "" creates."

Rhetorical Focus

Cause-and-Effect Organization

A **cause-and-effect essay** explains why certain actions, situations, or behaviors happen. The essay can start with an effect, such as success, and find its causes, which might be education or talent. Or the essay can begin with a cause and describe its effects.

Introduction
- The hook grabs the readers' attention.
- Background information helps the reader understand the cause(s) or effect(s). It can give historical information.
- The thesis statement shows the relationship between the cause(s) and effect(s).

Body Paragraphs
- The topic sentence in each paragraph defines a specific cause or effect to support the thesis statement.
- All supporting details must relate to the topic sentence. These details can include explanations, examples, or facts.
- Body paragraphs are organized in order of importance, chronologically, or according to short-term or long-term effects.
- Each paragraph must use clear logic.

Conclusion
- The conclusion restates the thesis.
- The conclusion may evaluate or reflect on the ideas presented.
- The conclusion may give advice or a warning.

Exercise 9 Reading a student essay

Read the essay. What are the effects of a positive outlook?

Effects of a Positive Outlook on Our Lives

Albert Camus once said, "Happiness is not a state to arrive at, rather, a manner of traveling." A positive outlook can help you be happy and change the outcome of your life. It can enrich your relationships, improve your health, and guide you through some of life's greatest challenges.

A positive outlook leads to happiness in professional, social, and personal relationships. Having a positive attitude will help you find a good job and keep it. In an article from *The Japan Times*, Edward Hoffman suggests, "For greater career satisfaction, notice your own peaks at work and then start planning how you can make these happen more often." He tells readers to focus on the positive in their work lives. Your co-workers will agree. Colleagues enjoy working with someone who always looks at the bright side and avoids conflict. Friends will appreciate your energy and want to spend more time with you, too. Unquestionably, a happy person makes everybody else happy. It is contagious. Happiness and a positive outlook can also have a beneficial effect on personal relationships. As a consequence, any partnership will be a solid, strong, and happy relationship.

Having a positive outlook also results in good health. In her article "How Attitude Affects Your Health," Dr. Deyanira Wong explains:

> The body releases stress hormones when people have negative attitudes. These hormones may cause temporary health problems such as headaches, upset stomach, or back pain. With long term stress and negativity, people may suffer from increased blood pressure, blood clots, insomnia, and chest pain associated with cardiovascular and heart disease. Attitudes may also have an effect on the body's immune system.

However, this can be avoided if people feel good about themselves. When you have a good sense of humor and laugh a lot, a chemical substance called serotonin is released into your bloodstream, giving you an immediate feeling of well-being and tranquillity. It has also been found that the elderly recover faster from illness when they are cheerful. Happiness directly impacts health and longevity.

Finally, people with positive outlooks are stronger and more capable of confronting difficult situations. They develop clear minds, which help them cope with life's challenges better than those individuals who are not at peace with themselves. Optimism creates the strength needed to find rational solutions to the many unexpected problems that life presents. This optimism also promotes self-esteem. For example, happier students are more likely to approach professors for help when they are having trouble in their course work. In contrast, unhappy students may internalize their frustrations and be less likely to seek help.

In conclusion, having a positive outlook and recognizing what makes you happy will bring harmony. Happiness will lead to strong relationships, good health, and the ability to face any obstacle. If you laugh more and think positively, you will change your life for the better.

Exercise 10 Examining the student essay

Examine the essay by responding to the questions and statements below. Then compare your answers with a partner.

1. Circle and label the hook. Why is a quotation a good way to start an essay?
   Cite something

2. Underline the background information.

3. Circle the thesis statement.

4. Underline the topic sentence in each body paragraph.

5. In body paragraph 1, according to Hoffman what can a person do to make his or her job more enjoyable? _make peaks at work longer_

6. In body paragraph 2, how does the quotation support the topic of the paragraph?
   Cited an article, statement

7. In body paragraph 2, why is the quotation indented? _To show it is_
   cited from someone

8. What two details from body paragraph 3 illustrate the effects of happiness?
   clear mind, optimism

9. How are the introduction and the conclusion similar? _They describe the_
   same point.

Exercise 11 Writing an outline

GO ONLINE

Review your brainstorming ideas and your freewriting exercise. Then go to the Web to print out an outline template for your essay.

In **Writing Process Step 3** you will . . .

- learn more about causes and effects.
- learn about sentence connectors showing cause and effect.
- write a first draft of your cause-and-effect essay.

Exercise 1 Reading a student essay

Read the essay. According to the writer, what factors lead to success in college?

Factors that Lead to Success in College

"I have sixty pages to read, a report to write, and I have to work tonight. I don't know how I'm going to make it through college!" one student complained to his roommate. This student's frustration is felt by many college students. The road to success in college is full of obstacles. Despite these obstacles, students can achieve their dream of earning their degree. They need support from family and friends, strong motivation, and the ability to focus.

Supportive families have a great impact on a student's success. Most students have families that protect and nurture them. Their family members act as helping hands, friends whom students can depend on emotionally. In an article discussing parent involvement in student success, authors Catherine Ratelle, Simon Larose, Frederic Guay, and Caroline Senecal suggest that parents can be supportive "by acknowledging their child's feelings" and by "encouraging them to form their own opinions." Students need this support system to help them realize their own abilities even when they doubt themselves. When the workload is too great or the exams are too difficult, students may get discouraged. This may result in their dropping out of school. However, families can encourage students to persevere. In addition, tuition and books are very expensive; consequently, some students are forced to work. If they receive financial assistance from their families, they can dedicate more time to their studies.

Students must keep up the motivation they need to study. Students have obligations to fulfill, such as completing homework assignments and research projects, studying for exams, and writing term papers. Many students work after school and arrive home late at night. Only dedicated and responsible students will push themselves to finish their work before going to bed. When the options are to go out with friends or stay home and work, only determined students will choose to study. And as Malcolm Gladwell says in his popular book *Outliers*, "Working really hard is what successful people do."

Students also need to focus on realistic academic goals. Many students are not aware of the importance of selecting the right college and major. In fact, a wrong decision may result in a waste of time and money. For example, some students may have very high expectations and may select majors that present demands they cannot meet. In some cases, they find themselves on a career path they do not even enjoy. As a result, they have to change their major or drop out of college when they realize that they cannot keep up their grades. If they are more focused on what they want, they will improve their chances of achieving their goals. "If you work hard and assert yourself and use your mind and imagination," according to Gladwell, "you can shape the world to your desires."

If students are enthusiastic about what they are studying, realistic about their academic goals, and receive support from their families, their college journey will be easier. They need to transform themselves into eagles. An eagle knows how to focus on what it wants and capture it even when the distance is great.

Respond to the essay by answering the following questions.

1. What are some of the obstacles that college students face?

   _____

   _____

2. According to the writer, what factors will lead to a college student's success?

   _____

   _____

3. How do the quotations in this essay support the writer's points?

   _____

   _____

4. Why is it important for students to be focused? _____

   _____

5. Do you agree with Gladwell's view on success? Why, or why not?

   _____

   _____

6. What obstacles and successes have you experienced in your academic life?

   _____

   _____

Rhetorical Focus

Relating Effects to Causes

A cause may have many effects, but they must be logically related. Read the following paragraph about the effects of a bus strike in a city. Notice how the writer crossed out a sentence that does not relate to the cause stated in the topic sentence of the paragraph.

> Bus strikes can disrupt the lives of residents in a city. When buses are on strike, many people are forced to find alternative means of transportation. Some may take taxis. However, during a strike it is often difficult to get a taxi. Other riders may create carpools to deal with the inconvenience. ~~Another effect is that public transportation can be very expensive~~. The worst effect is when workers cannot get to their jobs and lose much needed income.

The cost of transportation is not an effect of the strike and does not belong in the paragraph.

Exercise 3 Identifying related effects

Put a check (✓) next to the sentence that does not relate to the statement.

1. Being a happy person can benefit your life in many ways.
   - _____ a. A happy person can make friends more easily.
   - __✓__ b. There are many happy people all over the world.
   - _____ c. Happy people can solve their problems effectively.

2. It is important to get a college education.
   - _____ a. A college education provides more job opportunities.
   - _____ b. A person's life-long earning capacity is increased.
   - _____ c. Many colleges offer scholarships.

3. Air pollution has many negative effects.
   - _____ a. An example of air pollution is car-exhaust fumes.
   - _____ b. Asthma rates increase in highly polluted areas.
   - _____ c. Unclean air destroys the natural environment.

4. Watching too much television affects everyone.
   - _____ a. It reduces the amount of time people read.
   - _____ b. Research has shown that children become more aggressive.
   - _____ c. Many homes have more than one TV.

5. There are many advantages to using computers.
   - _____ a. Computers have become more reasonable to purchase.
   - _____ b. Using computers saves time writing reports and letters.
   - _____ c. The time needed to do research is greatly reduced.

Language and Grammar Focus

Cause Connectors
In a cause-and-effect essay, **connectors** create coherence by indicating the relationship between ideas in sentences.

Connectors Introducing a Clause
Use *because* or *since* to introduce a dependent clause. A dependent clause must be attached to a main clause to form a sentence.

When the dependent clause comes at the beginning of the sentence, it is followed by a comma. When it comes at the end of the sentence, no comma is used.

dependent clause	main clause
Because/Since the traffic was heavy,	we were late for class.

main clause	dependent clause
We were late for class	**because/since** the traffic was heavy.

Connectors Introducing a Noun Phrase

Use *due to, because of,* or *as a result of* to introduce a noun phrase.

A noun phrase is formed by a noun and its modifiers; for example, *heavy traffic.* It has no verb.

When the noun phrase comes at the beginning of a sentence, it is followed by a comma. When the noun phrase comes at the end of a sentence, no comma is used.

> Due to the **heavy traffic,** we were late for class.

> We were late for class due to the **heavy traffic**.

Exercise 4 Using connectors to introduce a clause

Combine each pair of sentences to show cause and effect. Use the connector in parentheses.

1. There have been new advances in air and space technology. We are able to travel greater distances in less time. (because)

   Because there have been new advances in air and space technology, we are able to travel greater distances in less time.

2. People are living longer. They are receiving better medical treatment. (since)

   Since _____

   _____

3. Orchestras are trying to attract a younger audience. Reduced rates at concert halls are available for many high school students. (because)

   _____

   _____

4. Research has shown that it reduces stress. More and more individuals are exercising. (since)   Since

   _____

   _____

5. Newspapers and magazines are losing subscribers. Readers obtain more up-to-date information from the Internet. (since)   Since

   _____

   _____

Exercise 5 Using connectors to introduce a noun phrase

Combine each pair of sentences to show cause and effect. Use the connector in parentheses. You will need to change the first sentence into a noun phrase.

1. Interest rates are low. More people are buying homes for the first time. (due to)

   Due to lower interest rates, more people are buying homes for the

   first time.

2. The pollen count is high. My allergies are very bad this season. (as a result of)

   As a result of the high pollen count, ✓,

3. My work was excellent. I received the highest grade in the class. (because of)   wordy

   Because of the excellence in my work; ✓

   ~~my excellent work,~~

4. The fire was destructive. The building had to be demolished. (due to)

   Due to the destructive fire, ✓

5. There is a great need for nurses. Many students are entering the profession. (due to)

   Due to a great need for nurses, ✓

6. The Suez Canal was built. Ships are able to travel faster from the west to the east. (as a result of)

   As a result of the Suez Canal, ✓

Language and Grammar Focus

GO ONLINE

Effect Connectors

Use *therefore*, *as a result*, or *consequently* to introduce effect clauses. These connectors always come between two main clauses. One clause shows a cause, and the other shows an effect.

When the clauses are joined into one sentence, the connector is always preceded by a **semicolon** and followed by a **comma**.

| cause | effect |

I studied all weekend for the test**;**   **as a result,** I got an A.

The connector may also begin a separate sentence. If so, it is followed by a comma.

| cause | effect |

I studied all weekend for the test.   **Consequently,** I got an A.

Exercise 6 Using connectors to show effect

Combine each pair of sentences to show cause and effect. Use the connector in parentheses.

1. The picnic was canceled. The weather was bad. (therefore)

   The weather was bad; therefore, the picnic was canceled.

2. The fire caused major damage to the school auditorium. We will have the performance in the town hall. (consequently)

   _____

   _____

3. Many people bought new homes. The economy began to improve. (as a result)

   _____

   _____

4. Flights no longer provide meals. Airlines have cut back services. (as a result)

   _____

   _____

5. The reviews were great. The theater added more performances. (therefore)

   _____

   _____

6. The exam was challenging. Many students failed. (therefore)

   _____

   _____

7. Cell phones are convenient and economical. Many people have cancelled their home service. (as a result)

   _____

   _____

Exercise 7 Writing a first draft

GO ONLINE

Review your outline. Then write your first draft of an essay on the causes or effects of an emotional, psychological, or physical condition. Go to the Web to use the Online Writing Tutor.

Exercise 8 Peer editing a first draft

GO ONLINE

A. After writing a first draft, it is helpful to get feedback on your ideas. Exchange essays with two other people. For each essay you read, answer the Peer Editor's Questions on a separate piece of paper. Then discuss your responses.

Peer Editor's Questions

1. What is your favorite part of the essay?

2. Are the causes or effects clearly stated? Explain.

3. What parts of the essay could be supported with more detail?

4. Are the paragraphs coherent or is there unnecessary information? Explain.

5. What suggestions would you make to help the writer improve the essay?

Go to the Web to print out a peer editor's worksheet.

B. Review your feedback and the organization guidelines on page 83. Make notes for your revision. In this step, you may add, remove, or rewrite information to clarify your ideas.

 In **Writing Process Step 4** you will . . .

- learn about real and unreal conditionals.
- edit your first draft.

Now that you have written a first draft, it is time to edit. Editing involves making changes to your writing to improve it and to correct mistakes.

GO ONLINE

Language and Grammar Focus

Conditional Sentences

Conditional sentences express cause and effect. A conditional sentence has a dependent *if* clause and a **main clause**. There are two types of conditional sentences: **real** and **unreal**.

Real Conditionals

Real conditionals express situations that may or may not happen. The *if* clause describes a possible condition or event. The main clause shows a possible result.

Use the **simple present** in the *if* clause of a real conditional. In the main clause, use the simple present, or a modal (*will, can, should,* or *may*) depending on how certain you are about the result. You may also use the imperative in the main clause to give an order.

When the *if* clause is first, use a comma. You may also use the word *then* before the main clause. When the main clause is first, do not use a comma.

> If I get the new job, (then) I will make more money.
> I will make more money if I get the new job.

In conditional sentences, either clause or both clauses can be negative.

> If I am not on time, I will take the bus.
> If I am not on time, I will not walk to work.

REAL CONDITIONALS		
⌐ *IF* CLAUSE ⌐		⌐ MAIN CLAUSE ⌐
IF + SIMPLE PRESENT	*(THEN)*	SIMPLE PRESENT
If I **leave** at 8:00,	(then)	I **catch** the bus.
IF + SIMPLE PRESENT	*(THEN)*	IMPERATIVE
If you **do not feel** well,	(then)	**stay** in bed.
IF + SIMPLE PRESENT	*(THEN)*	*WILL* FUTURE
If we **are** late,	(then)	we **will call** you.
IF + SIMPLE PRESENT	*(THEN)*	MODAL + MAIN VERB
If you **do not hurry,**	(then)	you **may be** late.

Exercise 1 Using real conditionals

Change each statement below into a real conditional sentence. Use *will*, *can*, *should*, or *may* in the main clause.

1. Take a computer course and have better job opportunities.

   If you take a computer course, you will have better job opportunities.

2. Study hard and pass the test.

   _____

3. Get a roommate and share the rent.

   _____

4. Go to bed early and wake up refreshed.

   _____

5. Read more and increase your vocabulary.

   _____

GO ONLINE

Language and Grammar Focus

Unreal Conditionals

Unreal conditional sentences express imaginary or hypothetical situations.
The *if* clause describes a condition or event that is not true at the time of writing.
The main clause shows the imaginary result of this condition.

Use the **simple past** in the *if* clause of an unreal conditional. In the main clause,
use *would*, *could*, or *might* with the main verb.

When the *if* clause is first, use a comma. When the main clause is first, do not use
a comma.

> If she studied harder, she would get better grades.
> She would get better grades if she studied harder.

UNREAL CONDITIONALS		
⌐ *IF CLAUSE* ¬		⌐ MAIN CLAUSE ¬
IF + SIMPLE PAST	*(THEN)*	*WOULD/COULD/MIGHT* + VERB
If I **had** a car,	(then)	I **would drive** to work.
If we **had** more money,	(then)	we **could buy** a car.
If I **had** more time off	(then)	I **might drive** to Saltillo.

Exercise 2 Using unreal conditionals

Write meaningful unreal conditional sentences. Use the words given.

1. snow in Hawaii / go skiing

   If it snowed in Hawaii, people could go skiing.

   _____

2. travel by bus / own a car

   _____

   _____

3. watch a lot of TV / read books

   _____

   _____

4. know how to cook / open a restaurant

   _____

   _____

5. become prime minister / give money to the poor

   _____

   _____

Exercise 3 Using real and unreal conditionals

Complete these sentences with your own ideas. Use commas where needed.

1. If the economy improves, *more people will have jobs.* _____

2. I would buy a beach house _____

3. If people receive better health care _____

4. I would learn a foreign language _____

5. If homeowners used solar energy _____

Exercise 4 **Editing a paragraph**

Read the paragraph. Correct six more mistakes in real and unreal conditionals.

>   If you ~~liked~~ _like_ music, think about taking a music appreciation course. If you would have any talent in that direction, you may want to join a choir. I joined a choir two years ago, and I enjoy it very much. I know that if I didn't have my rehearsals, I will be very unhappy. I look forward to working with a conductor, learning challenging pieces, and singing with a group. If I missed a rehearsal, I feel a little depressed. Even if we work on a difficult piece, I would find the challenge exhilarating. If music is not the hobby for you, you should found one that can bring you happiness. If you do, you would not be sorry.

Exercise 5 **Editing your first draft and rewriting**

Review your essay for mistakes. Use the checklist. Then write a final draft. Go to the Web to use the Online Writing Tutor.

GO ONLINE

Editor's Checklist

Put a check (✓) as appropriate.

CONTENT AND ORGANIZATION

○ 1. Does your essay have a thesis statement at the end of the first paragraph?

○ 2. Does each paragraph have a clear topic sentence and specific supporting details?

○ 3. Does the conclusion explain the outcomes?

LANGUAGE

○ 4. Did you use _will_ in the main clause for real conditional sentences?

○ 5. Did you use the simple past in the _if_ clause and _would, could,_ or _might_ in the main clause for unreal conditional sentences?

Go to the Web to print out a peer editor's worksheet.

 In **Review** you will . . .

• review the elements of cause-and-effect writing.

In Putting It All Together you will review the concepts you learned in this unit.

Exercise 1 Using cause-and-effect collocations

Complete the sentences by circling the correct preposition.

1. The reason (for / of) the student's success was the increase in class hours.

2. The outcome (from / of) the study showed that students were doing better in math.

3. A diet rich in fruit and vegetables can have a positive impact (in / on) your health.

4. Reviewing class assignments every night leads (in / to) academic success.

Exercise 2 Using correct punctuation with quotations

Read the following quotations and attributions. Add proper punctuation to identify the quotation and the attribution.

1. According to an old adage laughter is the best medicine.

2. Norman Cousins says laughter is a form of internal jogging.

3. Let us be grateful to people who make us happy, says Marcel Proust. He continues they are the charming gardeners who make our souls blossom.

4. Most people are about as happy states Abraham Lincoln as they make up their minds to be.

Exercise 3 Attributing quotations to their sources

Refer to the chart below to write sentences introducing each quotation and attributing the quotation to the author. Use a separate piece of paper.

QUOTATION	AUTHOR(S)	VERB/PHRASE
Remove the road blocks as you come across them. Otherwise you will have to climb a high mountain.	Master Jin Kwon	suggests
Let the beauty of what you love be what you do.	Jalal ad-Din Rumi	says
My humanity is bound up in yours, for we can only be human together.	Desmond Tutu	claims
Small opportunities are often the beginning of great enterprises.	Demosthenes	according to

Exercise 4 Identifying related causes and effects

Put a check (✓) next to the sentence that does not relate to the statement.

1. Strong economic growth in a country achieves many desired goals.

   _____ a. More people buy houses.

   _____ b. Strong economic growth followed World War I.

   _____ c. There is less unemployment.

2. Weather can influence your life.

   _____ a. Weather conditions in the world are changing.

   _____ b. Cool climates promote hard work.

   _____ c. In rainy climates people are often depressed.

3. Automobiles have changed the way people live.

   _____ a. They offer increased mobility.

   _____ b. Many cars have air-conditioning.

   _____ c. They save commuting time.

4. Good parenting has many positive effects.

   _____ a. Children treat others with respect.

   _____ b. It promotes academic success.

   _____ c. Good parenting takes a lot of time.

Exercise 5 Using connectors to show cause

Combine each pair of sentences with the connector in parentheses. You may need to change one of the sentences into a noun phrase.

1. The construction industry is thriving. There is a high demand for new housing. (since)

   _____

   _____

2. Many young adults go to college. The competition for jobs has become fierce. (because of)

   _____

   _____

3. People are living longer. Second careers are more common. (because)

   _____

   _____

Exercise 6 Using connectors to show effect

Combine each pair of sentences with the connector in parentheses.

1. People are cooking less. Microwaves are time saving. (therefore)

   _____

   _____

2. More police patrol the streets. Crime rates are high. (consequently)

   _____

   _____

3. Globalization is increasing. English has become a more popular language.
   (as a result)

   _____

   _____

4. Consumers have more choices. Shopping malls are huge. (consequently)

   _____

   _____

Exercise 7 Using real conditionals

Change the following statements into real conditional sentences.

1. Work hard and succeed in your career.

   _____

   _____

2. Work at a job you like and accomplish more in less time.

   _____

   _____

3. Travel around the world and learn about new cultures.

   _____

   _____

4. Purchase tickets online and save money.

   _____

   _____

Exercise 8 **Using unreal conditionals**

Write meaningful unreal conditional sentences. Use the words given.

1. play an instrument / join an orchestra

   _____

   _____

2. have a long semester / have less vacation time

   _____

   _____

3. marry a movie star / live in Hollywood

   _____

   _____

Exercise 9 **Editing a paragraph**

Read the paragraph, and edit as necessary. There are seven mistakes.

Today people work long hours and have too many responsibilities; as a result, they have very little leisure time. If people spent more time with family and friends, they will be happier. Often parents do not have enough time to spend with their children. Therefore, young children do not receive the parental attention they need. If parents have more home time, they could play games with their children and participate in more school activities. If parents spend more time with their children children would do better in school. Furthermore, if workers had more leisure time, they can go on more family vacations. Teenagers had more time to communicate with their parents if they did not have so many responsibilities. If leisure time increase, the family unit would be stronger, and society as a whole would benefit.

 In **Timed Writing** you will . . .

  • practice writing with a time limit.

Practice your test-taking skills with the following practice topic. Read the prompt. Then follow the steps below.

> Emotional stress is not a new phenomenon. However, people seem to be more stressed than ever. Write about the causes of stress in society today.

Step 1 BRAINSTORMING: 5 minutes

Write down ideas and vocabulary for your essay on a separate piece of paper.

Step 2 OUTLINING: 5 minutes

Write an outline for your essay. Use a separate piece of paper if necessary.

Introduction (First Paragraph)	
Hook Capture the reader's attention.	
Background Information Help the reader to understand the effect.	
Thesis Statement Clearly state the cause-and-effect relationship you will explore in the essay.	
Body Paragraphs (Middle Paragraphs)	
Topic and Controlling Idea Define one cause in each paragraph.	
Supporting Details Include explanations, examples, or facts to support each idea.	
Conclusion (Last Paragraph)	
Restatement of Thesis Evaluate or give advice.	

Step 3 **WRITING:** 40 minutes

Use your brainstorming notes and outline to write your essay on a separate piece of paper.

Step 4 **EDITING:** 10 minutes

When you have finished your essay, check it for mistakes using the checklist below.

GO ONLINE

Editor's Checklist

Put a check (✓) as appropriate.

○ 1. Does the introduction include a general thesis statement about the causes of stress?

○ 2. Does each body paragraph contain a topic sentence that defines a specific cause?

○ 3. Does the essay include connectors to show cause and effect?

○ 4. Are all the conditional verbs in the correct form?

○ 5. Does the conclusion restate the thesis?

Go to the Web to print out a peer editor's worksheet.

Write a cause-and-effect essay on one of the following topics.

Environmental Science: What are the causes of climate change? Is climate change a natural phenomenon? Could climate change be avoided by a change in human behavior?

Health: What are the health effects of exercising? How does exercise benefit people? When can exercise be harmful? Are there people who exercise too much? Explain.

Marketing: What are the effects of advertising on consumer purchasing? Do people purchase more after seeing attractive ads? Have people learned to ignore ads?

Medicine: What are the effects of medical technology on present-day society? Are there both negative and positive effects? If so, what are they?

World History: What were the effects of Gandhi's non-violent movement in India? Would this type of movement be effective in other countries? Why or why not?

UNIT 4

Argumentative Essays

Unit Goals

Critical Thinking Focus

- signal words used in argumentative essay assignments

Research Focus

- summarizing sources

Rhetorical Focus

- argumentative organization
- counter-arguments, concessions, and refutations

Language and Grammar Focus

- collocations associated with argumentative vocabulary
- connectors showing addition and contrast
- adverbial clauses
- noun clauses

As people grow, their views on ethical issues develop and change. Deciding what is right and what is wrong can be challenging. In this unit, you will explore and share your views on an ethical issue of importance to you.

Exercise 1 Thinking about the topic

A. Discuss the picture with a partner.

- Who are the two characters in this picture?
- What do you think is happening?
- Do you think the young man is guilty of a crime?

B. Make notes about the kinds of things people download off the Internet and whether or not you think downloading copyrighted property should be legal. Then discuss in small groups.

_____

_____

_____

_____

_____

_____

Many countries today are concerned about the ethics of downloading and sharing media from the Internet. The case of Yoshihiro Inoue may make some people think twice before engaging in this activity.

Japanese Man Found Guilty of Online Movie Theft

For the first time a Japanese court has found a man guilty of **piracy** and sentenced him to a year in jail. Yoshihiro Inoue, 42, downloaded movies off the Internet. He made copies of the movie *A Beautiful Mind* and then shared them with others. This is considered a crime in the U.S., Japan, and most other countries in the world. Inoue's case sets a **precedent** for anyone who distributes films illegally. His crime was stealing intellectual property. This kind of property, which is someone's creative invention, is protected by **copyright** law.

Today over eighty nations have copyright laws. These laws protect filmmakers, writers, photographers, and other innovative professionals. People who download and copy these works often do not understand or care about the financial loss to many of these artists. To protect artistic works within the U.S., the Copyright Act of 1976 was created. Most recently the Family Entertainment and Copyright Act of 2005 was signed into law. In addition, there are **treaties** and conventions to protect intellectual property between nations. One of these is the Universal Copyright Convention. Without these laws, piracy would go **unchecked.** Some of the many types of piracy include making DVDs, duplicating VHS tapes, using hand-held video cameras in movie theaters, and even receiving satellite signals without authorization.

Yoshihiro Inoue is not the first person to steal intellectual property, but he is the first to be charged with a crime for doing it. The movie industry in Hollywood and Asia are particularly interested in this case because they have a lot to lose. For a number of years the recording industry has **pursued** anyone downloading music from the Internet. Now the movie industry is following their example because piracy costs them almost $3 billion each year.

A major film costs about $80 million—$55 million to make and $27 million to advertise and market. Although many people believe that the film industry makes enormous profits, almost half of all films do not earn enough money to pay back their investors. If people continue to download movies off the Internet instead of paying to see them, the movie industry will have trouble surviving.

Adapted from "Japanese Man Jailed for Online Movie Piracy in Hollywood Crackdown." *Agence France Press* Dec. 2004. Print.

piracy: copying someone else's property illegally
precedent: an example for the future
copyright: legal ownership of a creative work

treaties: legal agreements between countries
unchecked: without notice
pursued: gone after

Exercise 3 Understanding the text

Write *T* for true or *F* for false for each statement.

_F_ 1. Inoue was an employee of a Hollywood studio.

_T_ 2. Copying movies is a crime in most countries.

_F_ 3. Inoue lost $80 million dollars in profits due to piracy.

_F_ 4. Copying and distributing movies has no effect on the movie industry.

_F_ 5. People who invest in movies always make money.

_F_ 6. The recording industry started prosecuting pirates before the movie industry did.

Exercise 4 Responding to the text

Respond to the reading by answering the following questions.

1. Why was this arrest important?

   He is the first one was arrested

2. What is the function of the Universal Copyright Convention?

   protect intellectual property.

3. Why is the movie industry concerned about people who download and share films?

   Because they will lost money

4. Do you think Yoshihiro Inoue should have gone to jail for Internet piracy? Explain.

   I think pay his fine is enough.

5. What kind of punishment do you think should be used against people who commit Internet piracy?

   A large fine

Exercise 5 Freewriting

Write for ten to fifteen minutes in your journal. Choose from topics below or an idea of your own. Express your thoughts and feelings. Don't worry about mistakes.

- According to the movie industry, people who download and distribute copyrighted materials should go to jail. What do you think of the movie industry's opinion on this issue?
- Describe an experience in which you had to persuade someone to agree with your position on an issue about which you were passionate.
- If somebody sells a product that is a copy of an original, who should be penalized: the buyer, the seller, or both? Explain your point of view.
- Evidence has shown that people who are bilingual have more advantages in life. How would you persuade a friend to start studying a second language?
- What are some of the advantages and disadvantages of working while attending school?
- What controversy in the news or in your community interests you? What is your opinion on the issue?

In **Writing Process Step 2** you will . . .

- learn how to analyze an argumentative assignment.
- learn about argumentative organization.
- brainstorm ideas and specific vocabulary to use in your writing.
- determine the audience and purpose for your argumentative essay.
- learn how to summarize a source.
- create an outline for an argumentative essay.

WRITING TASK Every day we are faced with ethical questions. Think about a topic for which you have a strong opinion. Argue in favor of or against the issue. Write your essay for the opinion page of a national newspaper. Defend your opinion with solid reasons, facts, and reliable outside sources. Your readers may disagree with your position; therefore, use strong evidence to refute any counter-arguments. Convince readers to support your opinion. Go to the Web to use the Online Writing Tutor.

Exercise 1 Understanding your assignment

Answer the following questions. Then compare your answers with a partner.

1. Circle the topic you are asked to write about. What are some ethical issues that interest you? _____

2. Underline the purpose of your paper. What should your essay accomplish?

   _____

3. What can you include in your essay to persuade readers who may not agree with your position? _____

Critical Thinking Focus

Signal Words Used in Argumentative Assignments

Review the vocabulary in your assignment. Notice the signal words related to an argumentative essay. Consider what the action verbs are asking you to do.

WORD	PART OF SPEECH	DEFINITION
argue	verb	to give reasons or cite evidence in support of an idea, action, or theory with the aim of persuading others
convince	verb	to succeed in making someone believe something or take action
defend	verb	to support a person or issue that is being criticized
oppose	verb	to disagree with someone's beliefs, actions, or plans, and to try to change or stop them
refute	verb	to prove that something is wrong
opinion	noun	a view or judgment formed about something
position	noun	a person's particular point of view or attitude toward something

Exercise 2 Identifying signal words in an assignment

A. Reread the writing task, and list words that signal an argumentative essay.

Capital punishment

B. Complete the following sentences with ideas you may use in your essay.

1. For a long time, I've held the **opinion** that _I support capital punishment_

2. I formed this **position** because _I think it is necessary for justice_

3. In my essay I might **argue** for _capital punishment exist_ _+s_

4. Readers who **oppose** my ideas might say that _it is not moral to execute it_

5. I can **refute** my opponents' ideas by explaining that _it is moral actually_

6. Another point I can use to **defend** my position is _it can discourage crime_

7. I would like to **convince** my readers to _support it_

Language and Grammar Focus

Collocations Associated with Argumentative Vocabulary

Some verbs used in argumentative assignments and essays are followed by objects or prepositions. Review the chart to see how they are used.

VERB	OBJECTS OR PREPOSITIONS	EXAMPLES
argue	that	The author of "Japanese Man Found Guilty of Online Movie Theft" **argues that** copyright laws protect filmmakers.
	for	Future filmmakers may **argue for** stronger copyright laws.
	against	The writer **argues against** downloading movies from the Internet.
convince	(someone) that	The author tries to **convince** readers **that** Internet theft is wrong.
	of	When I finished reading the article, I was **convinced of** the harm that Internet theft causes the movie industry.
	(someone) to	I wonder if the article will **convince** readers **to** pay for movies.
defend	against	The writer **defends against** the idea that filmmakers make huge profits.

Exercise 3 Identifying collocations with argumentative vocabulary

Circle the correct word in parentheses that completes the sentence.

1. Will the case of Yoshihiro Inoue convince readers (of / (to)) stop pirating materials with copyrights?

2. The movie industry argues (for / that) the world needs stronger copyright laws.

3. Many cable companies try to convince their customers (of / that) their service is worth the price.

4. Many musicians argue (for / that) increased protection of music websites.

5. Many young people today are not convinced (that / of) the severity of copying from other sources.

Exercise 4 Brainstorming ideas

A. **Choose an ethical issue that is important to you. Write the issue on the top line. Then write arguments in favor of or against the issue.**

ISSUE _____capital punishment_____

IN FAVOR	AGAINST
the red line · final punishment	violate human right
discouraging people crime	no one can deprive others life legally.
make up for victims can't	innocent problem
endless hate fix problem	

B. **Which side of the argument do you have the most support for? Write your essay from this point of view.**

In favor   human right

I believe some people who did something really bad should get this punishment as they ~~don't worth~~ are not worth reduction If there is a justice system to jude.

Exercise 5 Considering audience and purpose

A. Think about your audience. In this case they are readers of a national newspaper. How will they benefit from reading your essay? In the graphic organizer below, write notes about who you imagine will be reading your essay and how you hope they will respond to your ideas.

AUDIENCE	PURPOSE

B. Answer the following questions about your audience and purpose.

1. Considering the audience, how formal will this essay need to be?

_____

2. What will this audience already know about your topic?

_____

3. What do you want readers to believe or do after reading your essay?

_____

Exercise 6 Brainstorming vocabulary

Think about words you will need as you write about your ethical issue. Then make a Venn diagram like the one below. Write positive words and phrases on the left, negative ones on the right, and neutral ones in the middle. Use a dictionary or thesaurus to find more words you might need. The example here shows words about downloading copyrighted material from the Internet.

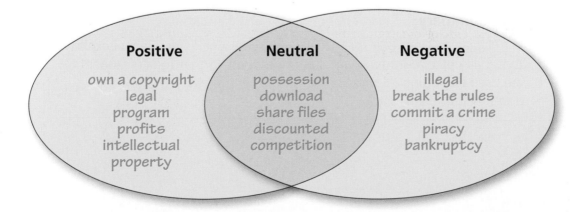

Positive
own a copyright
legal
program
profits
intellectual
property

Neutral
possession
download
share files
discounted
competition

Negative
illegal
break the rules
commit a crime
piracy
bankruptcy

Summarizing a Source

A **summary** is a shortened version of a source that strengthens an essay by giving it more substance. The source needs to be relevant to the topic.

When summarizing a source it is important to:

• understand the text you are summarizing.

• include only the most important concepts.

• use your own words.

• name the author and source.

Read the original article and the summary below. Notice how the summary writer is careful to use her own words. She also summarizes only the information that she needs to support her position. However, she does not misrepresent the information provided in the original text.

Original Text

Plagiarism Lines Blur for Students in Digital Age
By Trip Gabriel
August 1, 2010

A freshman copied and pasted from a Web site's frequently asked questions page about homelessness—and did not think he needed to credit a source in his assignment. . . . A student reprimanded for copying from Wikipedia in a paper on the Great Depression said he thought its entries . . . did not need to be credited since they counted, essentially as common knowledge. . . .

But these cases . . . suggest that many students simply do not grasp that using words they did not write is a serious misdeed. . . . Digital technology makes copying and pasting easy, of course. But this is the least of it. The Internet may also be redefining how students—who came of age with music file-sharing, Wikipedia, and Web-linking—understand the concept of authorship and the singularity of any text or image.

Original Source: *New York Times*

Effective Summary

In "Plagiarism Lines Blur for Students in Digital Age," Trip Gabriel explains that many plagiarism problems stem from the fact that today's students are used to getting information easily off the Internet, and they just don't realize it is wrong.

Exercise 7 Comparing the original text with the summary

Write the words used in the summary that correspond to the original text.

ORIGINAL TEXT	SUMMARY
students simply do not grasp that using words they did not write is a serious misdeed	Students don't know using words they didn't write is misdeed
digital technology makes copying and pasting easy	It is easy to copy and past easy due to digital technology

Exercise 8 Evaluating summaries

Read the original text and the summaries that follow. Use the evaluation criteria to discuss each summary with a partner. Circle the most effective summary.

Plagiarism is a violation of copyright laws. As a professor, I consider any copying or use of someone else's words or ideas without proper credit to be plagiarism. In my class, plagiarism will not be tolerated. Any form of plagiarism will automatically result in a failing grade, and I will send a letter of explanation to the college's academic judiciary committee. The judiciary committee will review the case to determine if legal action is necessary.

Source: Professor Victor Yazzi, Academic Writing 101, Vision College

EVALUATION CRITERIA	
An effective summary: • reports only the most important information. • reports information accurately.	• uses different words. • credits the source.

a. It is illegal to plagiarize. Students who copy other people's ideas will fail, and a letter will be sent to the judiciary committee for action.

b. According to Professor Yazzi of Vision College, plagiarism is illegal. He will fail anyone who steals from another person's ideas. He will also inform the judiciary committee.

name ... *article*

c. Plagiarism is illegal. People who plagiarize in Professor Yazzi's class will go to jail.

A. Read the text below, and circle the three most essential ideas.

Historian Who Chronicled the Roosevelts Admits Plagiarism

The historian Doris Kearns Goodwin is struggling to save her reputation after she admitted plagiarism. Ms. Goodwin, one the most popular and esteemed historians in America, has been vilified on editorial pages throughout the land. In happier times, Ms. Goodwin was a Pulitzer prize-winning chronicler of the Roosevelts and the Kennedys. . . . Her problems stem from the revelation that she lifted several passages of her 1987 bestseller, *The Fitzgeralds and the Kennedys*, from other authors. . . . She announced paperback copies of her book would be shredded and that her publishers, Simon and Schuster, would issue an edition that acknowledged the lifted passages. Ms. Goodwin also paid Ms. McTaggart some money. . . . Public television said she would take a break from *The News Hour with Jim Lehrer* program. The same day the University of Delaware withdrew an invitation for her to speak.

Source: Cornwell, Robert. "Historian Who Chronicled the Roosevelts Admits Plagiarism." *The Independent* 3 Mar. 2002. Print.

B. Summarize the passage.

_____

_____

_____

_____

_____

_____

_____

_____

_____

_____

_____

_____

Rhetorical Focus 🔍

Argumentative Organization

An **argumentative essay** is sometimes called a **persuasive essay.** This kind of essay expresses an opinion about a controversial issue. As the writer, you must take a position and persuade the reader to agree with your opinion by using strong, logical reasons to support your argument.

Introduction
- The hook gets the readers' attention.
- Background information gives a broader picture of the issue and why it is important. It can give details about the history of the people involved, what they want, and how the issue affects them.
- The thesis statement clearly states the writer's opinion about the issue.

Body Paragraphs
- The topic sentence in each body paragraph presents one distinct reason for the writer's point of view stated in the thesis.
- All supporting details in each paragraph must support the topic sentence. These details can be facts, examples, statistics, definitions, causes and effects, quotations, anecdotes, or summaries.
- The writer often presents an opposing opinion (a counter-argument). The writer may then express some agreement with the opposing view (a concession), but will show evidence that the writer's argument is stronger (a refutation).

Conclusion
- The conclusion restates the argument that appeared in the thesis.
- It can end with a prediction, a warning, or other type of comment that reinforces the writer's viewpoint.
- It may state the general issue in a broader context.

Exercise 10 **Reading a student essay**

Read the essay. What rules does the title refer to?

Breaking the Rules

A common question asks, "Why reinvent the wheel?" This question suggests that if work has already been done by someone else, there is no reason to redo it. For college students with heavy course loads, the question may be a tempting excuse for using other people's work. After all, surely someone has already written an excellent argumentative essay that can be downloaded easily from the Internet. The problem is that doing so is plagiarism, and it is irresponsible from a social and an academic standpoint.

Plagiarism is a violation of trust. Students are expected by teachers and their classmates to do their own work. When a student plagiarizes, he or she damages the relationship between the student and the teacher, as well as relationships with classmates. I remember when a student was discovered to have plagiarized his essay. We felt betrayed. Our classmate had lied to us. The essay had been printed in our school paper, and it was an embarrassment for everyone—the institution, the instructor, and the student—to discover that he had stolen another person's work.

Plagiarism is against the law. Even though buying essays and presenting them as your own may save time, this practice is illegal. Universities have developed ways to determine if students have plagiarized. Instructors can use software to compare a student essay with material on the Internet. This way, instructors can detect if a particular essay is original or a copied work. The consequences of plagiarism can be very serious in college as well as in future careers. According to an article in *The Independent*, a famous author and historian recently lost credibility when she plagiarized from her sources. The publishers had to reprint the book with an apology, and the author lost a position on a prestigious television program.

It is true that many college students have busy schedules and may have trouble completing their assignments on time. Some students may argue that because of their difficult situations, they sometimes have no choice but to buy essays off the Internet. However, buying essays off the Internet should never be the solution. Instead, students might try to negotiate the deadline with their instructor.

In "Plagiarism Lines Blur for Students in Digital Age," Trip Gabriel explains that a lot of the problems stem from the fact that today's students are used to getting information easily off the Internet, so they simply do not realize it is wrong. This may be true, but when it comes to buying essays from the Internet, it cannot be surprising to students that this is irresponsible.

Added to this is the problem that writing is a struggle for many students. They feel that their work may not get an A. It is this desire to do well that leads them to seek out illegal sources. They should realize that there are other options. They can go to a writing center for help. However, it is crucial that they do their own work. Otherwise, if they plagiarize, they will not develop their own writing and critical thinking skills.

I believe that university authorities and students should become more familiar with the drawbacks of plagiarism. Plagiarism damages classroom relationships. It violates school policies, and it prevents students from realizing their own potential. Plagiarizing is harmful to a student's academic success. When students plagiarize, they not only hurt others, but they lose out on their own education. Sacrificing one's education is certainly more costly than purchasing a $50 essay on the Internet.

Exercise 11 Examining the student essay

A. Respond to the essay by answering the following questions.

1. Why do some students plagiarize?

   Desire do well `busy

2. How would you describe the writer's opinion of people who plagiarize?

   Disagree strongly

3. According to the writer, what are some negative effects of plagiarizing?

   Damage the relationship with instructor, unable to critical thinking

4. Do you agree or disagree with the writer? Why?

   Yes, plagiadism is caused by lazy, if everyone being lazy, the society won't progress.

5. Did the writer influence your position? If so, which point influenced you the most?

   _No_

6. How does the writer use summaries in the essay? Are the summaries effective in supporting the writer's argument?

   Tell reader the consequence they may face, and warn everyone don't do that.

B. Examine the organization of the essay by responding to the questions and statements below. Then compare your answers with a partner.

1. Circle and label the hook. Is it effective in getting the readers' attention? Why or why not?

   Yes, it makes readers want to read the article.

2. Rewrite the thesis using your own words.

   It is irresponsible for students to plagiarism.

3. What kind of supporting details does the writer use in body paragraph 1?
   a. facts
   b. causes and effects
   c. statistics
   d. an anecdote

4. Underline the topic sentences in body paragraphs 1 and 2. How do these paragraphs support the essay's thesis?

   It is bad for plagiarism

5. What opposing ideas does the writer present in body paragraphs 3, 4, and 5? How does she argue against these ideas?

   busy · digital convenience · writing struggle

6. What is the writer's purpose for writing this essay? How do you know?

   Against plagiarism , thesis statement

7. How many reasons has the writer restated in her conclusion? Summarize these concluding ideas.

   3, violation of trust, against the law, irresponsible

Exercise 12 Writing an outline

GO ONLINE

Review your brainstorming ideas and your freewriting exercise. Then go to the Web to print out an outline template for your essay.

In **Writing Process Step 3** you will . . .

- learn about counter-arguments, concessions, and refutations.
- learn about connectors showing addition and contrast.
- write a first draft of your argumentative essay.

The consequences of plagiarism can be very serious in college as well as in future careers.

This may be true, but when it comes to buying essays from the Internet, it cannot be "irresponsible.

summery = cite

argue×2   assert   concludes

explain   emphasize

Exercise 1 Reading a student essay

Read the essay. Why does the writer think people should have free cable service?

Getting Free Cable

Everyone likes to watch TV. In fact, just one cable company in India has more than 80 million subscribers. In the United States, nearly 90 percent of the population has cable TV. However, cable service is overpriced, which has become a burden on many people. There is a cheaper alternative called digital satellite TV. Unfortunately this type of service is not available everywhere. Because viewers have limited options and because cable companies overcharge for their services, I believe that viewers have a right to use free, unauthorized cable service.

Cable companies charge a ridiculous amount for their services. For example, in the U.S. the family-plan package starts at about $80 per month, has a separate installation fee, and does not even include the movie channels. These packages consist of nine to eleven special movie channels. However, only two of the nine are usually worth watching. Most of the movies shown are old and tend to be constantly repeated. Consequently, customers are encouraged to get other packages to obtain the channels they want. There is one that includes phone services and cable for $100, but this discounted price is only good if you are a new customer. Once this initial period is over, the price for the same service increases more than $60 per month. The service is simply not worth paying for.

Satellite service is not a good alternative for viewers. Although it is cheaper, the quality is inferior. For example, images on TV may be disturbed by the weather. In addition, many buildings do not allow tenants to use satellite dishes because strong wind, snow, or rainstorms can knock down the dish and cause an accident. An individual cannot order satellite unless all, or at least a majority, of the tenants agree. Therefore, I see no other option than to use the cable signal illegally.

The Time Warner Cable website says that people may be stealing the signal actively or passively. Time Warner explains that passively stealing happens when you move into a location that gets cable without an account and you use it without contacting the company. Time Warner complains that not only are they losing money, but the quality of service to their other customers suffers. Most importantly they insist that obtaining free cable is unlawful. I understand their point of view. However, life has simply become too expensive, and a number of people, including myself, are willing to take desperate measures to get free service. We feel that these companies have a monopoly. Because there is only one cable company in each area, the company has no competition and can charge what it wants. This is not fair.

In conclusion, I think that people should be allowed to use unauthorized cable service unless we have reasonable options. The legal options we have now are not good enough since cable is overpriced and satellite TV is inferior or not available. Unless cable companies lower their fees, they will lose more and more paying customers. They will eventually put themselves out of business.

Exercise 2 Examining the student essay

A. Respond to the essay by answering the following questions.

1. What reasons does the writer give for using unauthorized cable service?
   Too expensive , monopoly

2. According to the writer, what are some of the problems with satellite service?
   Not stable , need every tenants agree

3. What arguments do cable companies have against using unauthorized cable service?
   lost money

4. What flaws do you see in the writer's opinion? _This is not a reason to use unauthorized cable service_

B. Examine the organization of the essay by responding to the questions and statements below. Then compare your answers with a partner.

1. Underline the thesis. What opinion does it give? _free unauthorized cable service_

2. How does the background information help readers understand the writer's opinion? _It can let us know how many people use it_

3. What facts does the writer use to support his argument? _the monopoly - high percentage_

4. Does the summary of Time Warner's opinion support the essay's position? Why or why not? _He is opposite to writer's opinions but the author utilize it to argue, support his idea._

5. What prediction does the writer make in the conclusion? _If company doesn't lower it's price, it will lose more money._

Rhetorical Focus

Counter-Argument, Concession, and Refutation

The goal of an argumentative essay is to convince the reader of the writer's point of view. To make an argumentative essay strong, the writer includes a **counter-argument**, a **refutation**, and a **concession**.

• The counter-argument is the opposing point of view. By including the counter-argument, the writer shows an understanding of opposing viewpoints.

• In a concession the writer agrees that the opposing point of view is valid but emphasizes how his or her argument is still stronger.

• The refutation is the writer's response to the counter-argument. In the refutation, the writer shows why the counter-argument is weak and his or her position is strong.

Counter-argument	Some students may argue that because of their difficult situations, they sometimes have no choice but to buy essays off the Internet.
Concession	I understand that students are under a lot of pressure to produce well-written essays to pass their classes, but this does not justify plagiarism.
Refutation	If they plagiarize, they will not develop their own writing and critical thinking skills.

Exercise 3 Identifying refutations and concessions

Write *R* for each argument showing a refutation and *C* for each item showing a concession.

_R_ 1. Some students photocopy chapters of books that are required for their courses. They believe that they are justified because textbooks are so expensive. Not only is this illegal, but it also shows a lack of intellectual integrity.

___ 2. Manufacturers often justify copying famous designer articles such as handbags and jewelry because they can sell these items far below the cost of the original. Many consumers cannot see any difference, and they benefit from paying lower prices. If consumers benefit, this practice should not be illegal.

___ 3. Musical performers often use copyrighted songs for their shows. They complain about having to pay royalties and fees to the copyright owners. Since musicals are performed in front of small audiences and the performers do not make much money, it seems unfair for them to pay high fees just to sing a song.

___ 4. Some producers have taken other peoples' story lines for movies and adapted them for their own films. They argue that their version is significantly different from the idea first presented to them. However, this practice is unethical and dishonest; therefore, the original creator should be compensated.

___ 5. Robert's brother Jerry helped Robert write a college term paper a few years ago. Now Jerry feels that he has the right to submit the same term paper for his college course. Even though Jerry helped write Robert's report, Jerry is not the original author. He should not assume that he can get credit for writing the paper.

___ 6. A pastry chef working in a cupcake bakery learned new recipes from the café's head baker. When the pastry chef opened his own cupcake shop in another neighborhood, he insisted on using the same recipes he had used at his previous job. He was wrong to take recipes created by another baker and use them in his new business.

Exercise 4 Developing refutations and concessions

Write a refutation or concession giving your opinion of each issue.

1. Some Web developers believe it is okay to use images they found on the Internet to make their own webpages more attractive.

_____

_____

_____

2. Many drivers fail to stop for red traffic lights when they see that no one is coming in the opposite direction.

_____

_____

_____

3. Some students think they should be allowed to use unlicensed software for educational purposes.

_____

_____

_____

Language and Grammar Focus

Connectors to Show Addition and Contrast

To construct a strong argument, it may be necessary to provide additional information or to contrast different pieces of information. **Addition and contrast connectors** link ideas between two main clauses and clarify the relationships between ideas.

Connectors That Show Addition

Use the connectors *furthermore, in addition,* or *moreover* to indicate additional information.

When the clauses are joined in one sentence, the connector is always preceded by a semicolon and followed by a comma.

> The U.S. created the Copyright Act of 1976 to protect artistic works**; in addition,** there are treaties to protect intellectual properties between nations.

An addition connector may also begin a separate sentence. In this case it is followed by a comma.

> The U.S. created the Copyright Act of 1976 to protect artistic works. **Moreover,** there are treaties to protect intellectual properties between nations.

Connectors That Show Contrast

Use the connectors *nevertheless* or *however* to show contrast.

When the clauses are joined in one sentence, the connector is always preceded by a semicolon and followed by a comma.

> Students who struggle with their writing might be tempted to plagiarize**; however,** it is crucial that they do their own work.

A contrast connector may also begin a separate sentence. In this case it is followed by a comma.

> Students who struggle with writing their papers might be tempted to plagiarize. **However,** it is crucial that they do their own work.

Exercise 5 Using connectors for addition or contrast

Combine the two sentences with a connector to indicate additional information or contrast. Check your punctuation carefully.

1. Patents are important because they protect the inventions of individuals. They are generally good for only 20 years.

   <u>Patents are important because they protect the inventions of individuals;</u>

   <u>however, they are generally good for only 20 years.</u>

2. Once an invention is patented, only the owner can make, sell, or distribute the product. Anyone else who wants to profit from this item must get permission from the owner.

   _____

   _____

3. Novels, plays, newspapers, and other original printed materials are protected by copyright law. Visual images such as drawings, photographs, and cartoons are still illegally copied off the Internet.

   _____

   _____

4. The U.S. Congress passed the Family Entertainment and Copyright Act of 2005 to counter piracy. The English Parliament created the Digital Economy Act for the same reason.

   _____

   _____

5. Many consumers try to keep up with modern technology. This is almost impossible because what is popular today becomes obsolete tomorrow.

   _____

   _____

Exercise 6 Writing a first draft

GO ONLINE

Review your outline. Then write your first draft of an argumentative essay about an ethical issue of interest to you. Go to the Web to use the Online Writing Tutor.

Exercise 7 Peer editing a first draft

GO ONLINE

A. After writing a first draft, it is helpful to get feedback on your ideas. Exchange essays with two other people. For each essay you read, answer the Peer Editor's Questions on a separate piece of paper. Then discuss your responses.

Peer Editor's Questions

1. What position is the writer taking?

2. What is the writer's strongest support for the position?

3. What is your favorite part of this essay?

4. Is the essay persuasive enough to change a person's opinion? Why or why not?

Go to the Web to print out a peer editor's worksheet.

B. Review your feedback and the organization guidelines on page 117. Make notes for your revision. In this step, you may add, remove, or rewrite information to clarify your ideas.

 In **Writing Process Step 4** you will . . .

- learn about adverbial clauses.
- learn about noun clauses.
- edit your first draft and write a final draft.

Now that you have written a first draft, it is time to edit. Editing involves making changes to your writing to improve it and to correct mistakes.

Language and Grammar Focus

Adverbial Clauses

An **adverbial clause** is a dependent clause. It is always attached to a main clause. Just as **adverbs** modify verbs, adverbial clauses modify the verb of the main clause to show time, place, reason, or purpose.

All adverbial clauses must contain a subordinator (a word linking the adverbial clause to the main clause), a subject, and a verb.

The adverbial clause can come before or after the main clause, but the punctuation is different. Use a comma after an adverbial clause when it begins a sentence.

adverbial clause	main clause

While summers are hot in Dubai, they are cool in Oslo.

main clause	adverbial clause

Summers are cool in Oslo **while they are hot in Dubai.**

Adverbial Clauses to Show Contrast and Concession

To make your argumentative essay as persuasive as possible, you will need to contrast two points of view effectively. You will also need to make concessions to opposing points of view. Use adverbial clauses to show contrast or concession.

Begin an adverbial clause with *while* or *whereas* to show contrast. The information in the adverbial clause comes in opposition to the information in the main clause.

> **While** some people like to invest their savings, most people prefer to keep their money in saving accounts.

> Some students rely on buying essays off the Internet **whereas** others believe it should never be an option.

Begin an adverbial clause with *although* or *even though* to show concession. The information in the adverbial clause presents a concession to the information in the main clause.

> **Although** satellite service is cheaper than cable, the quality is inferior.

> Some students buy essays and present them as their own **even though** it is illegal.

Exercise 1 Using adverbial clauses to show contrast or concession

Add a main clause to the following adverbial clauses to create sentences that show contrast or concession. Check your punctuation carefully.

1. while some people prefer to buy name-brand products

   While some people prefer to buy name-brand products, others choose

   generic brands because they are cheaper.

2. whereas some people like to go to a movie theater

   _____

   _____

3. even though soccer is the most popular sport in Argentina

   _____

   _____

4. while shopping online is very convenient

   _____

   _____

5. although air travel is expensive

   _____

   _____

GO ONLINE

Language and Grammar Focus

Noun Clauses

Noun clauses are dependent clauses that function as nouns in a sentence and are connected to a verb phrase. They have a subject and a verb but do not express a complete idea by themselves.

I believe **what he told me.** I demand **that he apologize.**

Noun Clauses with *What*

We can use noun clauses that begin with *what* to express thoughts or opinions.

A noun clause with *what* can be the subject or object of a sentence.

| subject | object |

What he told me is not true.   I do not believe **what he told me.**

Noun Clauses with *That*

Noun clauses with *that* can be used to express an opinion or give a recommendation.

Noun clauses with *that* can follow a verb phrase or an adjective.

That can generally be omitted.

> I believe **(that) the meeting will go ahead.**

When the noun clause follows the adjectives *important, crucial, mandatory, vital,* or *essential* or the verbs *suggest, advise, demand, insist, propose, argue,* or *recommend,* the verb in the noun clause is always in the base form.

> It is <u>vital</u> that you **finish** the job by Wednesday.
> I <u>suggest</u> she **wear** a different dress to the interview.

Exercise 2 Identifying noun clauses

A. Underline the noun clause in each sentence. Then circle the verb phrase in the main clause.

1. It (is crucial) that companies pay their employees promptly.

2. What they decided to do is ridiculous.

3. It is essential that you check the painting's authenticity.

4. We advise that you buy jewelry only from a reputable dealer.

5. The board demands that the school hire master teachers.

6. I don't agree with what he said.

B. Look back at the student essay on pages 122–123. Find sentences with noun clauses. Then write the sentences on a separate piece of paper.

Exercise 3 Creating noun clauses

Complete each unfinished sentence so that it has the same meaning as the statement printed above it. Use noun clauses with *that*.

1. The students want the college to add new math courses to the curricula.

   The students think _that the college should add new math courses to_
   the curricula.

2. The city residents want the mayor to lower the fare for public transportation.

   The city residents recommend _____

   _____

3. The community should provide after-school programs for teenagers.

   Parents believe _____

   _____

4. The government must offer free health care for all citizens.

   It is crucial _____

   _____

5. Most employers want their workers to arrive on time.

   Most employers insist _____

   _____

Exercise 4 Editing a paragraph

Read the paragraph. Correct the mistakes in adverbial and noun clauses. There are four more mistakes, including one punctuation mistake.

Identity theft occurs when someone steals your name, social security number, or credit card number and uses it for his or her own purposes. Although most people feel safe from identity theft, thousands of people each year fall victim to this new form of crime. We recommend that you to protect yourself from this hideous crime. Do not disclose personal information to strangers. Destroy all unused bank and credit card statements. Keep an eye on your credit cards. Although credit cards make life easier you need to be cautious when using them. In case you become a victim of identity crime, follow these steps. We advise that you should file a police report as soon as you realize that something is wrong. It is crucial that you to notify your credit card companies and banks immediately. We also suggest that you could keep records of all your documents in a safe place. Therefore, if you become a victim, you will have all the necessary information to facilitate the filing process.

Exercise 5 Editing your first draft and rewriting

Review your essay for mistakes. Use the checklist. Then write a final draft. Go to the Web to use the Online Writing Tutor.

GO ONLINE

Editor's Checklist

Put a check (✓) as appropriate.

CONTENT AND ORGANIZATION

○ 1. Did you include a thesis statement that identifies your position?

○ 2. Do your body paragraphs include topic sentences that support your position?

○ 3. Did you include a counter-argument and a refutation?

○ 4. Does your conclusion restate the thesis in different words and convince your readers of your position?

LANGUAGE

○ 5. Did you use adverbial clauses to show contrast and concession?

○ 6. Did you remember to use a comma when your adverbial clauses appear at the beginning of a sentence?

○ 7. Did you use any noun clauses with *what* or *that*?

○ 8. Did you remember to use the base form of the verb in noun clauses after certain noun adjectives and verbs?

Go to the Web to print out a peer editor's worksheet.

 In **Review** you will . . .

- review collocations associated with argumentative vocabulary.
- practice writing an effective summary.
- review the use of counter-arguments, concessions, and refutations.
- practice using connectors to add information and to show contrast.
- practice using noun clauses and adverbial clauses.

In Putting It All Together you will review the concepts you learned in this unit.

Exercise 1 **Identifying collocations with argumentative vocabulary**

Circle the correct word in parentheses that completes the sentence.

1. Authors argue (that / against) they should be compensated when their work is used in other publications.
2. Artists need to convince the public (to / that) buy original works.
3. Fashion designers defend (that / against) false labeling on imitations.
4. Scientists are convinced (that / of) the need for enforcing patent laws.

Exercise 2 **Writing summaries**

Read the original text, and write a summary below.

Years ago a cruel joke suggested that President Ford couldn't chew gum and walk at the same time.

Silly, of course, but it turns out that there was a bit of truth in it. Not just for Mr. Ford, but for all of us.

Any time we try to perform two things at once, one performance suffers, albeit only slightly when it comes to nearly brainless tasks like walking and chewing at the same time. The going gets tough, though, when either task becomes more demanding.

Take talking on a cell phone while driving a car, for example, and this is not part of an anti-cell phone crusade. New research shows, however, that the price we pay for trying to listen intensely comes at the expense of our ability to see clearly.

When we turn the "listening knobs" up, says psychologist Steve Yantis of Johns Hopkins University, we turn the "visual knobs" down.

It doesn't make any difference if the phone is hands-free. It's the listening that makes the difference, not the nature of the instrument.

Source: Dye, Lee. "Why Cell Phones and Driving Don't Mix" *ABC News* 29 Jun. 2005.

_____

_____

_____

_____

Exercise 3 Identifying refutations and concessions

Write *R* for each refutation and *C* for each concession.

_____ 1. Many people like using the Internet on smartphones. However, others find the screen so small that it is annoying.

_____ 2. Movie companies use music recorded in the 1940s and 1950s but do not pay for permission to use it. This seems reasonable since this music is so old.

_____ 3. Too many consumers think it is acceptable to use credit cards to buy more than they can afford. Unfortunately, if they continue to overspend year after year, they will become hopelessly in debt.

_____ 4. Even though some parents think it is a nuisance to put children into special car seats, research has shown that car seats save many lives.

Exercise 4 Using connectors to show addition and contrast

Combine the two sentences with a connector to indicate additional information or contrast. Check your punctuation carefully.

1. Many companies copy the ingredients found in famous perfumes. Other companies steal patterns for dishware, sheets, and towels.

   _____

   _____

2. Many college students know that plagiarism is illegal. Websites that sell essays continue to grow. _____

   _____

   _____

3. Writing a research paper takes time and patience. It takes determination.

   _____

   _____

4. Media-related property theft has resulted in legal retaliation. The number of individuals illegally obtaining media online has increased.

   _____

   _____

   _____

Exercise 5 Using adverbial clauses to show contrast or concession

Add a main clause to the following adverbial clauses to create sentences that show contrast or concession. Check your punctuation carefully.

1. Although people in Japan greet each other by bowing _____

   _____

   _____

2. While opponents say that television has too much violence _____

   _____

   _____

3. Whereas many people go on vacation in the summer _____

   _____

   _____

4. Even though cell phone users believe that they have the right to talk whenever and

   wherever they want _____

   _____

   _____

Exercise 6 Creating noun clauses

Complete each unfinished sentence so that it has the same meaning as the statement printed above it. Use noun clauses with *that*.

1. Cyclists in Australia wear helmets.

   It is mandatory _____

2. A driver should check the car's oil and tires before taking a long trip.

   It is essential _____

3. The taxpayers want the mayor to build a new highway.

   The taxpayers propose _____

4. College students should have their own computers.

   Colleges recommend _____

Exercise 7 Editing a paragraph

Read the paragraph and edit as necessary. There are eight mistakes.

To complete a research project on the Internet, it is important that you must find a good search engine. There are many available some are better than others. Once you have chosen your search engine, it is essential that you should narrow your search to a specific topic. Type in the keywords for your search. We recommend that you will check your spelling carefully. If you misspell too many words, you will not get the right results. As soon as you have your list of websites, we suggest that you quickly to scan the list. Some people choose websites randomly, others find that the first five to ten sites listed are usually the best. Be prepared to look at a lot of websites before you find what you need. Open the sites, and skim them to find out if the information will work for your project. It is tempting to copy the material that you have found, it is mandatory that you to use your own words when you write your paper. You should include the website address in your notes.

 In **Timed Writing** you will . . .

- practice writing with a time limit.

Practice your test-taking skills with the following practice topic. Read the prompt. Then follow the steps below.

> Write an argumentative essay on whether or not you think technologies such as cell phones, computers, and DVDs benefit society. Before you begin to write, review the suggested time management strategy below.

Step 1 **BRAINSTORMING:** 5 minutes

Write down ideas and vocabulary for your essay on a separate piece of paper.

Test-Taking Tip

Be sure to take only one position. Add a counter-argument, but don't argue both sides.

Step 2 **OUTLINING:** 5 minutes

Write an outline for your essay. Use a separate piece of paper if necessary.

Introduction (First Paragraph)	
Hook Capture your reader's attention.	
Background Information Give the reader a broad picture of the issue and why it is important.	
Thesis Statement Clearly state your position on the issue.	
Body Paragraphs (Middle Paragraphs)	
Reasons and Controlling Ideas Present reasons that support your position.	
Supporting Details Include facts, examples, statistics, definitions, questions, and a counter-argument.	
Conclusion (Last Paragraph)	
Restatement of Thesis Restate the thesis and provide a prediction, a warning, or another comment to reinforce your viewpoint.	

Step 3   WRITING: 40 minutes

Use your brainstorming notes and outline to write your essay on a separate piece of paper.

Test-Taking Tip

Before you revise and edit your essay, look back at the prompt, your brainstorming notes, and your outline to be sure you didn't forget important ideas.

Step 4   EDITING: 10 MINUTES

When you have finished your essay, check it for mistakes using the checklist below.

GO ONLINE

> ## Editor's Checklist
>
> **Put a check (✓) as appropriate.**
>
> ○ 1. Do you have a thesis statement that takes a clear position?
>
> ○ 2. Do the body paragraphs include distinct reasons to support your position?
>
> ○ 3. Does the third body paragraph contain a counter-argument and a refutation?
>
> ○ 4. Did you use connectors that show contrast or addition?
>
> ○ 5. Did you use noun clauses correctly?
>
> ○ 6. Did you use adverbial clauses correctly?
>
> ○ 7. Does your conclusion repeat the reasons in your argument?
>
> **Go to the Web to print out a peer editor's worksheet.**

Write an argumentative essay on one of the following topics.

Education: Argue for or against getting your college degree through online courses. How effective are online courses? Is it better to have face-to-face contact with other students and instructors? Do online courses give more people access to education?

Health: Argue for or against a vegetarian diet. Is a vegetarian diet healthful? Should people avoid meat to save animal lives? What effect would vegetarianism have on the environment?

History: Argue for or against having history as a required course. What do people actually learn from history courses? Will this information help them with their careers? Why or why not?

Marketing: Argue for or against advertising on the Internet. Does advertising on the Internet work? Do people respond to Internet advertisers? Are ads intrusive to serious Internet users?

Psychology: Argue for or against children's use of video games. Do video games teach children violent behaviors? Do they teach skills? Do video games lead to antisocial behavior?

Sociology: Argue for or against reducing the number of hours people work per week. Should companies require workers to work no more than 40 hours per week? How would this affect economic growth? How would it affect family life and the emotional health of workers?

UNIT 5

Classification Essays

Academic Focus | Career Planning

Unit Goals

Critical Thinking Focus
- reading and analyzing bar graphs

Research Focus
- paraphrasing a bar graph

Rhetorical Focus
- classification organization
- establishing order of importance, degree, and size

Language and Grammar Focus
- gerunds and infinitives
- verbs following *make*, *let*, and *have*

Dealing with masses of information is a part of everyday life. To process this information more easily and to make it more manageable, we often create categories. In this unit, you will classify the talents and skills you possess that will help you succeed academically and professionally.

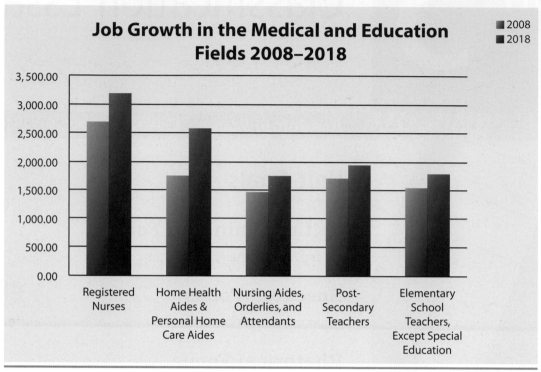

Source: U.S. Bureau of Labor Statistics. GPO.

Exercise 1 Thinking about the topic

Discuss the graph with a partner.

- Which occupations show the largest job growth? What do you think is causing this growth?
- Which two job categories show almost the same growth?
- Compared to 2008, approximately how many more post-secondary teachers are needed for 2018? What may be contributing to this growth?
- According to the graph, how many more post-secondary teaching positions are there in 2018 as compared to nursing aids, orderlies, and attendants?

In this article, Steve McCormack explains the advantages of having employability skills for entering the workforce. According to Mr. McCormack, which soft skills will people need?

Learn Soft Skills to Gain a Tougher Edge in the Job Market

There used to be a time, a few decades back, when anyone with a degree could more or less be guaranteed a job: perhaps not their dream job, but certainly something to get started in the world of employment. But as more young people started to go to university, that certainty began to **recede**, and we approached the stage where a master's-level qualification was regarded as the minimum requirement to secure that first job.

Now, however, the reality is that, even a **sheaf** of academic qualifications does not guarantee automatic entry to employment. Graduates, however well qualified, also have to be able to demonstrate a set of what are called employability skills to show they can **hit the ground running** in the workplace. These include all-round communication skills, the ability to work in a team and to be a self-starter, to be **versatile,** and to have a creative approach to problems.

The need for universities to pass these skills on to students has been spotted by the UK Commission for Employment and Skills (UKCES), the government agency charged with raising the workplace skill levels of the population as a whole.

In a recent report it **bemoaned the fact** that too many universities and colleges neglect to teach employability skills or, for funding or capacity reasons, found it difficult to develop them.

Cass Business School at London's City University is one of the schools that include employability skills as part of the learning experience. Every student in a Cass course has a "relationship manager" within the Cass careers department, who guides the student through a program of sessions designed to land a job and **thrive** once a job has started.

Topics covered include the art of **cold-calling,** something not only useful in the pursuit of job interviews, but also in carrying out the duties of a job itself. Likewise, the "influencing and persuading sessions" at Cass try to give students these soft skills that they can **deploy** once in a job, as well as in the job search.

"These skills are very important because it's not like 20 years ago when most master's students came with a view to moving on to a Ph.D.," says Andrew Clare, associate dean with responsibility for all postgraduate programs at

Cass. "Today, they want to get the background that will help them get a job."

To bring a real working-environment atmosphere to Cass students, the university insists that all course work be done in groups. They frequently place students with peers they don't really know and who come from another part of the world.

At the University of Plymouth's Business School, all undergraduate and post-graduate programs highlight key employability skills, including communication, application of IT, numeracy and literacy, teamwork, and business awareness. For the school's associate dean, Hilary Duckett, presentation skills are particularly important: "We use every opportunity we can to engage students' presentation skills in a real setting. We find that it **galvanizes** their capabilities when they have to make presentations to real clients."

And, given the increasing competition among universities for fee-bearing students, Duckett concedes that stressing the employability credentials of courses is essential these days.

"This has always been relevant for business school, but now it is increasingly important, and it is part of the sell to potential students."

Adapted from McCormack, Steve. "Learn Soft Skills to Gain a Tougher Edge in the Job Market." *The Independent* 31 Mar. 2011.

recede: diminish
sheaf: bundle or stack
hit the ground running: be prepared to start something immediately
versatile: able to adapt; flexible
bemoaned the fact: regretted
thrive: prosper, flourish
cold-calling: phoning someone you don't know
deploy: use
galvanizes: stimulates

Exercise 3 Understanding the text

Write *T* for true or *F* for false for each statement.

_____ 1. The writer believes that a master's degree is essential for finding a good job.

_____ 2. Communicating well is an important skill for the future.

_____ 3. Cass Business School guarantees employment for all its students.

_____ 4. Many master's students today don't get a Ph.D.

_____ 5. Cold-calling is only good for getting a job interview.

Exercise 4 Responding to the text

Respond to the reading by answering the following questions.

1. How have hiring practices changed in the job market?

    _____

    _____

2. What are some of the employability skills?

    _____

    _____

3. What is the role of the "relationship manager" at Cass Business School?

    _____

    _____

4. According to Andrew Clare, why are soft skills important?

    _____

    _____

5. How does Cass Business School simulate the real working environment?

    _____

    _____

    _____

6. Why are presentation skills essential?

    _____

    _____

Exercise 5 Freewriting

Write for ten to fifteen minutes in your journal. Choose from topics below or an idea of your own. Express your thoughts and feelings. Don't worry about mistakes.

- Write about a profession that intrigues you.
- What steps are you taking to achieve your professional goals?
- Write about a project that you have completed in a group.
- What are some of your academic strengths?
- The jobs of the future will require technical and other important skills. What skills and talents do you possess?
- How would you categorize your extracurricular activities?

In **Writing Process Step 2** you will . . .

- learn how to organize a classification essay.
- brainstorm ideas and specific vocabulary to use in your writing.
- determine the audience and purpose for your classification essay.
- learn to analyze and paraphrase a bar graph.
- create an outline for a classification essay.

WRITING TASK Sorting information makes it more manageable and meaningful. It allows us to prioritize the categories we select. In this unit you will write an essay to a college or graduate school classifying the abilities and talents you possess that will make you a successful candidate for their program. Include descriptions, definitions, examples, and statistics. Go to the Web to use the Online Writing Tutor.

Exercise 1 Understanding your assignment

Respond to the questions and statements about the Writing Task.

1. Underline the type of essay you will write.
2. What abilities and talents do you have, and how can they be categorized?

   _____

   _____

3. What is the purpose of this essay? _____

   _____

4. What details should you include to support your thesis? _____

   _____

   _____

5. Who is your audience? _____

Exercise 2 Brainstorming ideas

Fill in the chart below with the names of three professions that interest you. Next to each profession list the abilities you possess for that profession.

Profession	Abilities

Exercise 3 Considering audience and purpose

A. Think about your audience. Who are these people? What are some of the categories you expect to be evaluated on? In the chart below, describe the people you imagine would read this essay. Which academic disciplines might they represent? What experiences and abilities would this audience expect to find in a successful candidate?

AUDIENCE	CATEGORIES OF ABILITIES AND EXPERIENCES

B. Answer the following questions about your audience and purpose.

1. Considering the audience, how formal will this essay need to be?

   _____

2. What does your audience need to learn from your essay?

   _____

   _____

3. Which category do you think will impress your audience the most?

   _____

Exercise 4 Brainstorming vocabulary

Classify your abilities from Exercise 2 using the chart below. Add additional abilities to the chart.

LEADERSHIP	PROBLEM-SOLVING	CREATIVITY	INTERPERSONAL SKILLS	KNOWLEDGE
confidence				

Reading a Bar Graph

Writers often include statistics in their academic essays to substantiate their ideas. Some of these statistics may come from **bar graphs**.

Vocabulary for Reading Bar Graphs

title	The title appears at the top of the graph and names what will be compared.
vertical axis	The vertical axis is on the left of the graph. It usually shows the value of what is being compared.
horizontal axis	The horizontal axis runs along the bottom of the graph. It usually gives the names of what is being compared.
scale	The scale is a range of values used to measure data.
bars	Bars are rectangular blocks on either axis.
key	The key identifies the bars.

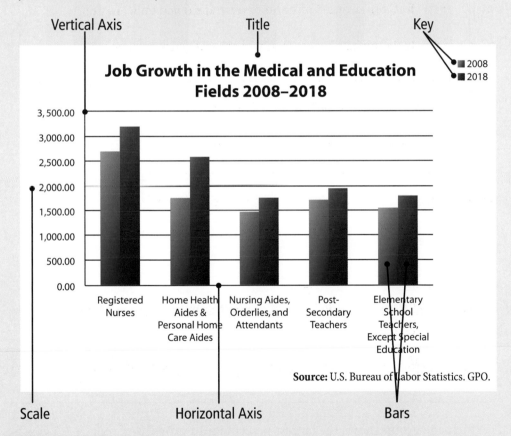

Analyzing a Bar Graph

Analyzing graphs is one way of gathering data. Here are some guidelines.

• Compare the data.

• Notice similarities and differences between and among the groups.

• Identify the groups that have the most extreme differences between them.

Read the bar graph. Then answer the questions below.

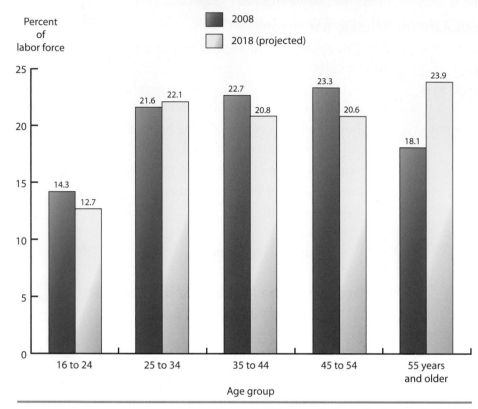

Percent of Labor Force, by Age Group

Source: BLS Division of Industry Employment Projections

1. What is the graph title? _____

   _____

2. What information does the horizontal axis contain? _____

   _____

3. What does the key tell you? _____

   _____

4. Which age group shows the largest percentage of growth? _____

5. Which age group shows the smallest percentage of growth? _____

6. Which age groups shows a decline in workforce in 2018? _____

Paraphrasing a Bar Graph

When you **paraphrase,** you put information into your own words. To support ideas in an essay with information you find in a graph, you will need to paraphrase the graph so that your readers can interpret how the information applies to your thesis.

When you paraphrase a graph, it is important to:

• include the source.

• mention what is being measured.

• state the most relevant statistics related to your essay.

• discuss any significant trends.

The example below is an effective paraphrase of the graph on page 149:

> According to the U.S. Bureau of Labor Statistics, jobs for registered nurses will increase by 500.00 by 2018, while home health care and personal home care aides will see an increase of 750.00. In the educational field, which includes elementary and post-secondary teachers, an increase of 200.00 is expected through 2018.

Exercise 6 Paraphrasing a bar graph

Read the following paraphrase of the graph on page 150. Fill in the missing information.

The bar graph from the Bureau of Labor Statistics indicates how

changes in _____*age*_____ groups will affect the number of people in the
　　　　　　　　1.

_____ _____. The graph shows that the oldest group
　　2.　　　　　　　　3.

will have the _____ percentage of increase among the groups.
　　　　　　　4.

They will show a _____ difference between 2008 and 2018.
　　　　　　　　5.

The only other group to experience an increase will be the _____
　　　　　　　　　　　　　　　　　　　　　　　　　　　6.

age group. The 35–44 age group and the 16–24 age group will have almost

_____ percentage of decrease, with the youth population
　　7.

decreasing by _____ percent over the 2008–2018 period.
　　　　　　　8.

The graph suggests that older people will be working longer and not retiring.

Read the bar graph below. Paraphrase the graph on a separate piece of paper.
Include the title, what is being measured, and the most significant findings.

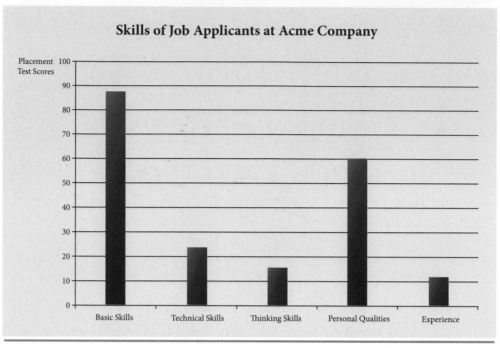

Source: Acme Company

Rhetorical Focus 🔍

Classification Organization

In a **classification essay,** information is organized into meaningful categories or
groups, and each follows a single, unifying principle.

Introduction
- The hook catches the readers' attention.
- Background information includes a general statement or statements that give a
  broad picture of the subject matter to be discussed.
- The thesis statement contains the topic and the controlling idea for the whole
  essay. It tells what is classified and how it is organized.

Body Paragraphs
- One category or group is described in each paragraph. The information is
  ordered logically. For example, it can be organized in order of importance or in
  chronological order.
- A topic sentence in each paragraph describes the category or group. It supports
  and expands the thesis statement.

- The supporting details can be paraphrases, definitions, examples, anecdotes, statistics, or quotations that elaborate on the topic sentence.
- The concluding sentence of each paragraph may either bring the idea of the paragraph to a close or suggest the content of the next paragraph.

Conclusion
- The conclusion presents a new way of stating the thesis.
- It delivers a prediction, gives advice, makes a general statement, or proposes a question to keep the audience thinking about the subject.

Exercise 8 Reading a student essay

Read the essay. According to the writer, what careers will have the most growth in the near future? *health service, education, information technologies, communication*

Jobs of the Future

Where will the jobs of the future be? Many students who are not certain about their career path may be asking this question. If you are already sure what field you want to work in, it is still useful for you to know the occupational outlook for employment opportunities in that field. Because people often change careers throughout their lives, it is important to continuously assess the employment outlook of the future. Health services, education, information technologies, and communications are expected to have the highest levels of growth in the number of people employed over the next decade.

Health services and education comprise the sector with the highest growth rate. Under the umbrella of health services are health care and social assistance, which include public and private hospitals, nursing and residential care facilities, and individual and family services. Those in personal care and human-services occupations should be able to listen to and understand verbal communication and most importantly communicate written information and medical instruction to their clients. Employment growth will be driven by the increasing demand of the aging population. According to the U.S. Bureau of Labor Statistics, jobs for registered nurses will increase by 22.2 percent by 2018, while home health care and personal home-care aides will see a 47 percent increase. In the educational field, which includes elementary and post-secondary teachers, a 15 percent increase is expected through 2018. Rising student enrollments at all levels of education will increase demand and new job opportunities for educational services.

Today, information technology comprises the second fastest growing sector of the worldwide economy. Network systems, data communication analysts, and computer software engineers will be in demand. The proliferation of jobs is driven by the increasing reliance of businesses on information technology and the continuing importance of maintaining systems and network security. These are the best career opportunities for people with a bachelor's or master's degree in engineering or science. Personality types most suitable for these professions are investigative in nature since these jobs require people to search for facts and to analyze data. In other words, these occupations require the ability to work with ideas and to solve problems.

The third highest percentage of growth will take place among communication-related industries such as software publishing, Internet publishing, broadcasting, and wireless telecommunication careers. These are highly desirable and attractive career options for people with a bachelor's or master's in business administration or the humanities. The information sector also includes motion picture production and publishing of newspapers, magazines, or books. People who have special artistic talents and enjoy working with computers will find these professions very rewarding. There will also be a significant demand for telecommunication services, cable services, high-speed Internet connectors and software, all of which will fuel job growth among these industries.

In summary, the fastest growing careers for the 21st century will be in occupational areas related to health and human services, education, information technologies, and communications. We live in an information age where speed and knowledge, as well as interpersonal relationships and the ability to provide needed human services, are the essence of life. All these occupations and skills represent the vital force that drives the economy.

Exercise 9 Examining the student essay

A. Respond to the essay by answering the following questions.

1. What skills are needed for entering human-service occupations?

   _____

   _____

2. Why are information technologies growing so rapidly?

   _____

   _____

3. What qualities are useful for work in industries related to communications?

   _____

   _____

4. What degrees are recommended for people entering computer-related industries?

   _____

   _____

B. Examine the organization of the essay by responding to the questions and statements below. Then compare your answers with a partner.

1. Circle the sentence(s) that make up the hook.
2. Underline the thesis statement.
3. According to what principle are the categories being grouped? _____

   _____

   _____

4. What is the category for body paragraph 1? _____

   _____

   _____

5. How do the statistics support the topic of body paragraph 1? _____

   _____

   _____

6. How do we know these statistics are reliable? _____

   _____

   _____

7. The writer concludes his essay with—
   a. a prediction.   b. advice.   c. a general statement.

Exercise 10 Writing an outline

GO ONLINE

Review your brainstorming ideas and your freewriting exercise. Then go to the Web to print out an outline template for your essay.

 In **Writing Process Step 3** you will . . .

- learn to categorize groups.
- learn about the organizing principles of importance, degree, and size.
- write a first draft of your classification essay.

1. The job in the future ? health care, information technology

Corey

Exercise 1 Reading a student essay

Read the essay. According to the writer, why is it important to know your personality type? *It may help you find the idea job.*

Does Your Career Choice Fit Your Personality?

My grandmother once said, "Find a job that you like, and you'll never have to work a day in your life." Choosing the right career may in fact be connected to knowing your personality type. Personality typing can help people find the career path they are best suited for. The original research in this area was done by the psychologist Dr. Carl Jung and was greatly expanded by Katherine C. Briggs and Isabel Briggs Myers who created the Myers Briggs Personality Test. This test can help people understand their personality traits, which may influence their career choices. The Myers Briggs Personality Test identifies sixteen personality types; this essay will focus on the most analytical.

The ENTJs (Extroverted, iNtuitive, Thinking, Judging) are natural leaders who value knowledge and are future-oriented. They possess excellent communication skills and are self-confident and decisive. Intuitive and insightful, these people use their environment as their source of energy. They make decisions in a methodical and systematic way. Some suitable professions for ENTJs are lawyers, bankers, financial advisors, entrepreneurs, and computer consultants.

INTJs (Introverted, iNtuitive, Thinking, Judging) understand complex theories because they can see the bigger picture. They are insightful, and they follow their intuitions rather than simply accepting what others say. They are extremely logical, rational, and original. They like working independently, and they excel in strategizing. INTJs are best suited for careers as scientists, engineers, medical doctors, corporate strategists, or systems analysts.

ENTPs (Extroverted, iNtuitive, Thinking, Perceiving), whose dominant functions are extroversion and intuition, are project-oriented, creative, and logical. They are flexible in facing new challenges. These exuberant people motivate others around them with their high energy and warm personalities. As information seekers, ENTPs are able to grasp abstract ideas and solve complex problems. Suitable professions for this personality type include law, psychology, sales, and business.

INTPs (Introverted, iNtuitive, Thinking, Perceiving) seek both truth and knowledge. They are independent, original, and often eccentric. These types don't follow the crowd and are sometimes viewed as being detached from society. INTPs often choose careers in the foreign service, journalism, real estate, technical fields, or advertising.

According to IQTestNow.com, understanding how jobs match temperaments can improve a person's future. Recruitment specialists using three of the most reliable psychological tests, including the Myers Briggs Personality Test, depicted in their graph the distribution of sixteen personality types found in society. Not so surprising is the fact that Mahatma Gandhi represents the protector type, and Albert Einstein is a thinker. What is both astonishing and comforting is that a majority of people fit into the category of philanthropists. Taking a personality test can be very beneficial to you both in making choices around your career and in determining how to understand people of other personality types.

Exercise 2 Examining the student essay

A. Respond to the essay by answering the following questions.

1. Why is it important to understand your personality type?

   It can help people to make choices around career.

2. What is the underlying principle of the personality types chosen for the essay?

   ENTJs / most analytical

   means why did the author
   choose to discuss
   4/16 personality types

3. How would you compare introverts and extroverts?

Good at expressing, speaking or not

4. In dealing with people, how are ENTJs and ENTPs similar?

extroverted, good at communication

5. Why is science a good field for INTJs and INTPs?

They follow ~~theitselves~~ rather than follow others
themselves

6. Which character traits do you identify with?

INTJs

B. Examine the organization of the essay. Then respond to the questions and statements below. Compare your answers with a partner.

1. What type of hook does the writer use?

   a. a question   b. a quotation   c. an anecdote

2. What is the writer's thesis statement?

The Myers Briggs Personality Test, identifies sixteen personality
Types; this ···· analytical

3. What background information does the writer give about personality tests?

help people understand their trait · career ✗

4. How does the writer organize the categories?

Different personality types — not enough info

5. What information does the writer paraphrase?

Know more yourself by this test, more likely to find
the idea job ✗

6. The writer concludes the essay with—

   a. a restatement of the benefits of personality tests   ✗
   b. a prediction of how personality tests will be used in the future
   c. a question to help readers think more about the subject
   d. a warning that people should not rely so much on personality tests

Language and Grammar Focus

Classification of Groups

When writing a classification essay, establish meaningful and logical categories using similar characteristics, qualities, or functions. The groupings should also share a single underlying principle to preserve unity.

One **principle of classification** for archivists, publishers, and librarians is *people who work with books*. Archivists, publishers, and librarians all belong to that group.

Exercise 3 Classifying with groups

Select the occupations from the box to create three specific groups with common characteristics. Then write a principle of classification for each group.

park ranger A	interpreter B	civil engineer C
linguist D	landscaper E	surveyor F
architect G	farmer H	speech therapist J

1. **Group 1:** _park ranger, farmer, landscaper_

   Principle of Classification: _about nature_

2. **Group 2:** _linguist B Speech therapist, interpreter_
   surveyor

   Principle of Classification: _about communication_

3. **Group 3:** _civil engineer, architect, surveying_

   Principle of Classification: _about building action_

Language and Grammar Focus

Establishing Order of Importance, Degree, and Size

Once you have created categories for your classification essay, you will need to organize the information in a logical way. Arranging facts in order of importance, degree, or size will help you establish useful hierarchies. Compare the two examples below.

Example 1 — An important skill for succeeding as a teacher is the ability to communicate ideas. Another important skill is the ability to break down information. Computer skills are also important.

Example 2 — **The most important skill** needed to succeed in teaching is the ability to break down information. **The second most important skill** is the ability to communicate ideas. Computer skills are useful but are **the least important** ability needed to be a teacher.

In the first example, the information is presented in no particular order. However, in the second example, the writer uses expressions to organize the ideas in order of importance. As a result, the second example shows greater clarity and coherence.

The following expressions will help you rank objects or ideas in order of importance, degree, or size:

the most/greatest	the second most/greatest	the least/fewest
the fastest	the second fastest	the slowest
the best	the next best	the worst
the highest	the second highest	the lowest
the largest	the second largest	the smallest
the maximum		the minimum
the most significant		the least significant
the most important		the least important

The highest percentage of the total number of teachers work in elementary schools. **The second highest** amount teach in junior high schools and high schools. **The lowest** number of teachers work in adult education.

To show similarity or equality, use *the same, almost the same,* and *similar to.*

The skills needed to succeed in some professions are **the same**.
The artistic abilities of fine artists are **similar to** those of photographers.

Exercise 4 Using expressions that show importance or similarity

Study the graph about working hours in different countries. Then complete the sentences with the phrases from the box below. You may use the same phrase more than once. In some cases several options are possible.

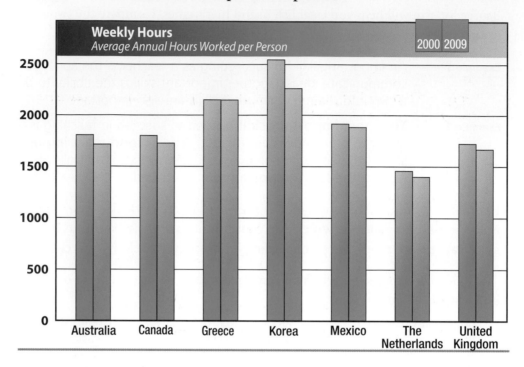

| the most significant | almost the same | the smallest | the greatest |

1. Greece had <u>almost the same</u> number of working hours in 2000 and 2009.

2. The countries that had _____ amount of change between 2000 and 2009 were Greece and Mexico.

3. Korea had _____ decrease from 2000 to 2009.

4. Greece and Korea had _____ number of working hours in 2009.

5. Canada and Australia had _____ number of working hours in 2009.

6. Of all seven countries, The Netherlands had _____ number of working hours in 2009.

7. Korea had _____ number of working hours of all seven countries both in 2000 and in 2009.

Exercise 5 **Writing a first draft**

GO ONLINE

Review your outline. Then write your first draft of a classification essay about the abilities and talents you possess that will make you a successful candidate for a college or graduate program. Go to the Web to use the Online Writing Tutor.

Exercise 6 **Peer editing a first draft**

A. After writing a first draft, it is helpful to get feedback on your ideas. Exchange essays with two other people. For each essay you read, answer the Peer Editor's Questions on a separate piece of paper. Then discuss your responses.

GO ONLINE

> ## Peer Editor's Questions
>
> 1. What would you like the writer to explain in the background?
>
> 2. What qualities is the writer classifying? Are these clearly stated?
>
> 3. Did the writer provide enough information to make you feel that he or she will be a successful student?
>
> 4. What was your favorite part of the essay? Why?
>
> 5. What two suggestions would you give to the writer for how to improve the essay?
>
> **Go to the Web to print out a peer editor's worksheet.**

B. Review your feedback and the organization guidelines on pages 152–153. Make notes for your revision. In this step, you may add, remove, or rewrite information to clarify your ideas.

 In **Writing Process Step 4** you will . . .

- learn about gerunds and infinitives.
- study verbs following *make, let,* and *have.*
- edit your first draft and write a final draft.

Now that you have written your first draft, it is time to edit. Editing involves making changes to your writing to improve it and to correct mistakes.

Language and Grammar Focus

GO ONLINE

Gerunds

A **gerund** is an *-ing* form of a verb that acts like a noun. It can be used in a sentence to name an activity or a situation.

A gerund can be one word (*eating*). It can also be part of a longer phrase with an adverb (*eating quickly*), with a noun (*eating dinner*), or with a prepositional phrase (*eating in a restaurant*).

All verbs, except modal verbs, have gerund forms.

Gerunds Following Verbs

A gerund can act as the subject of a sentence.

> **Eating dinner** in a five-star restaurant can be expensive.

A gerund can also be an object and follow a verb. Some common verbs that can be followed by gerunds are *enjoy, consider, like, dislike, practice, prefer,* and *recommend*.

> I <u>like</u> **eating dinner** late.

Gerunds Following Prepositions

Gerunds can follow prepositions such as *about, for, on,* or *in*.

One common pattern of gerunds following prepositions is *be* + adjective + preposition + gerund. Some examples of this pattern that a gerund may follow include *be concerned about, be involved in, be good at, be responsible for, be accustomed to, be interested in,* and *be nervous about*.

> I <u>am interested in</u> **acquiring** new skills.

Exercise 1 Identifying gerunds

Underline the gerunds in the following sentences. Write *S* if the gerund is the subject or *V* if it follows the verb.

___S___ 1. <u>Piloting</u> a plane involves good judgment.

___V___ 2. Nutritionists suggest eating fresh fruits and vegetables.

___S___ 3. In addition to talent, being a professional musician demands commitment.

___V___ 4. Radiology technicians practice taking X-rays.

___S___ 5. Learning a foreign language is rewarding.

___S___ 6. For many students, studying abroad is a life-changing experience.

Exercise 2 Using gerunds in sentences

Complete each sentence with a gerund. Compare your answers with a partner.

1. We discussed _changing the schedule._

2. I always enjoy _sleeping_

3. _____ can be a wonderful experience.

4. Many people dislike _going to school_

5. _Playing soccer_ is a useful skill to learn.

6. If you want to feel better, you should avoid _feeling bad again_

Exercise 3 Using gerunds after prepositions

Complete the following sentences with the gerund form of the verbs in the box.

memorize	discover	predict	take	improve	research

1. Meteorologists are responsible for _predicting_ the weather.

2. Politicians are often concerned about _improve_ the community.

3. Actors are good at _memorize_ their scripts.

4. Historians are accustomed to _research_ the lives of world leaders.

5. Astronomers are interested in _discover_ new galaxies.

6. Students are nervous about _take_ exams.

Write sentences using the phrase in parentheses and a gerund.

1. (be accustomed to) <u>I am accustomed to staying up late.</u>

   _____

2. (be interested in) _____

   _____

3. (be nervous about) _____

   _____

4. (be responsible for) _____

   _____

5. (be concerned about) _____

   _____

GO ONLINE

Language and Grammar Focus

Infinitives

An **infinitive** is formed with *to* + the base form of the verb. An infinitive can be used in place of a noun to describe an activity expressed by a verb.

An infinitive can be part of a longer phrase with an adverb (*to drive quickly*) or a noun (*to drive a car*).

All verbs, except modal verbs, have an infinitive form.

Infinitives after Verbs

An infinitive can follow a verb or the object of a verb. In some cases the object of a verb can be omitted.

Verbs that follow the verb + infinitive pattern include *agree, appear, decide, learn, like, plan,* and *seem*. Some verbs such as *like* can be followed by a gerund or an infinitive.

> I <u>like</u> **to eat** out on Tuesday nights.

Verbs that follow the verb + object + infinitive pattern include *advise, allow, cause, get, hire, invite, order, require, teach,* and *tell*.

> The counselor <u>advised</u> Thomas **to take** a biology class.

Verbs that follow the verb + (object) + infinitive pattern include *ask, choose, expect, need,* and *want*.

> I <u>want</u> **to go** home.
> I <u>want</u> you **to go** home.

Exercise 5 Writing sentences with infinitives

Rearrange the words and phrases below to make complete sentences. Use correct punctuation.

1. arrive / the principal / to / on time / the teachers / expected

   The principal expected the teachers to arrive on time.

2. new employees / to / is planning / hire / the company

   _____

3. to / next year / graduate / expects / Barbara

   _____

4. to / require / their medical exams / all hospitals / pass / doctors

   _____

   _____

5. a foreign language / we / to / learn / decided

   _____

6. dress appropriately / job applicants / employment agencies / to / for their interviews / advise

   _____

   _____

Exercise 6 Completing sentences with infinitives

Complete each sentence with an infinitive. Remember to use an object where needed. Compare your answers with a partner.

1. The professor agreed *to give us an extra day to finish our assignments.*

2. The police officer asked _____

3. My doctor advised _____

4. The mayor needs _____

5. My friend wants _____

6. Many children learn _____

Language and Grammar Focus

Verbs Following *Make, Let,* and *Have*

The verbs *make, let,* and *have* are followed by an object and the base form of a verb, not the infinitive. The objects of these verbs perform the action expressed by the base form.

> She **made** her son <u>clean</u> his room.
>
> **x** She made her son to clean his room. (INCORRECT).

Exercise 7 **Using *make, let,* and *have***

Complete the following sentences using *make, let,* or *have* and a verb in the base form.

1. The principal of the high school ___had the students attend an assembly.___

2. My parents _____

3. The lifeguard _____

4. The judge _____

5. The bus driver _____

6. The airlines _____

Exercise 8 **Editing a paragraph**

Read the paragraph. Correct the mistakes in gerund and infinitive forms. There are six more mistakes.

Finding
   Find the right career may seem like an overwhelming task for many. If you are looking for job opportunities, you need take enough time to explore all the options. Begin by assess your skills. Decide what you are good at doing and what you enjoy. Are you interested in designing or creating things with your hands? Perhaps you are more accustomed to sit at a computer. Do you like working indoors, or do you enjoy be outside in nature? Some people prefer work on a team, whereas others dislike working with colleagues. This may be the most important decision you will ever make, so explore your talents and abilities carefully, and do not let anyone to influence you.

Exercise 9 Editing your first draft and rewriting

Review your essay for mistakes. Use the checklist below. Then write a final draft.
Go to the Web to use the Online Writing Tutor.

GO ONLINE

> # Editor's Checklist
> **Put a check (✓) as appropriate.**
>
> ### CONTENT AND ORGANIZATION
>
> ○ 1. Does your introduction include enough background information
>   to help your readers understand your topic?
>
> ○ 2. Does your thesis statement have a unifying principle?
>
> ○ 3. Do your body paragraphs support your thesis?
>
> ○ 4. Does your conclusion restate the thesis in new words and provide
>   something for readers to think about?
>
> ### LANGUAGE
>
> ○ 5. Did you use gerunds correctly?
>
> ○ 6. Did you use the correct pattern for infinitives following objects?
>
> ○ 7. Did you use the correct word pattern for the verbs *make, let,* and *have*?
>
> **Go to the Web to print out a peer editor's worksheet.**

 In **Review** you will . . .

- practice expressions of importance, degree, size, and similarity.
- practice analyzing and paraphrasing a bar graph.
- review using infinitives and gerunds.
- practice classifying in groups.
- practice editing.

In Putting It All Together you will review the concepts you learned in this unit.

Exercise 1 **Reading and analyzing a bar graph**

Read the bar graph. Then answer the questions below.

Average hours spent per day in leisure and sports activities, by youngest and oldest populations

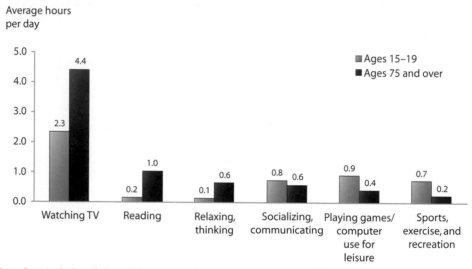

Average hours per day

■ Ages 15–19
■ Ages 75 and over

Note: Data includes all days of the week and are annual averages for 2009.

Source: Bureau of Labor Statistics

1. What does the scale measure? _____

   _____

2. What leisure activity do people engage in the most? _____

   _____

3. How would you rank the order of activities that young people engage in?

   _____

   _____

4. Which two activities does the older group spend an equal amount of time on?

   _____

Exercise 2 Using expressions that show importance or similarity

Reread the information in the graph about leisure activities. Then complete the sentences with the phrases from the box below.

the least   the most significant   the same   the smallest   the second highest

1. The oldest and youngest segments of the population have _____
   _____ difference in terms of socializing and
   communicating.

2. Teens spend _____ number of hours reading as the
   older group spends on sports and exercise.

3. Teenagers spend _____ amount of time relaxing and
   thinking.

4. The elderly spend _____ number of hours reading.

5. _____ difference between the youth and the elderly is
   in the time spent watching television.

Exercise 3 Paraphrasing a bar graph

Write a paraphrase of the bar graph on page 170. Make sure to include the title, what is being measured, and the most significant findings.

_____

_____

_____

_____

_____

_____

_____

_____

_____

_____

_____

_____

Exercise 4 Using verbs followed by gerunds

Complete the following sentences with the gerund form of one of the words in the box.

form	arrive	practice	write	prepare	receive

1. Chefs enjoy _____ unusual meals.

2. The heads of state considered _____ an alliance.

3. Bankers dislike _____ complaints from their customers.

4. _____ at the airport two hours before departure is recommended.

5. Many authors prefer _____ directly on a computer rather than with pen and paper.

6. _____ many times before performing helps musicians.

Exercise 5 Choosing the correct preposition

Write the correct preposition from the box to follow the adjective in each sentence.

for	in	to	about	at	with

1. Doctors are accustomed _____ working long hours.

2. Lawyers are good _____ arguing a case.

3. Archeologists are interested _____ digging for fossils.

4. Police are responsible _____ protecting the community.

5. Conservationists are concerned _____ saving our forests.

6. Investors are nervous _____ losing their money.

Exercise 6 Choosing the correct verb

Choose the correct verb to complete the following sentences.

1. My professor _____ me to take a writing course.
   a. let
   b. advised
   c. made

2. My boss _____ me to leave early.
   a. allowed
   b made
   c. had

3. The librarian _____ the children to be quiet.
   a. let
   b. had
   c. expected

4. The director _____ the actor repeat the scene.
   a. had
   b. asked
   c. told

5. The coach _____ the team play an extra game.
   a. wanted
   b. expected
   c. let

Exercise 7 Using the base form or the infinitive form

Circle the correct form of the verb in parentheses.

1. The pilot had the passengers (fasten / to fasten) their seat belts.

2. The security guards did not allow anyone (enter / to enter) the building without identification.

3. The chairman of the board did not expect his entire staff (attend / to attend) the business meeting.

4. The law firm made the paralegals (work / to work) overtime.

5. The student did not want his classmates (read / to read) his essay.

Exercise 8 Classifying with groups

Select the countries from the box to create three specific groups with common characteristics. Then write the principle of classification for each group.

Australia	Morocco	Peru	United Kingdom	Uruguay
Brazil	Libya	Saudi Arabia	United States	

1. Group 1: _____

   Principle of Classification: _____

2. Group 2: _____

   Principle of Classification: _____

3. Group 3: _____

   Principle of Classification: _____

Exercise 9 Editing a paragraph

Read the paragraph and edit as necessary. There are eight mistakes.

There are many good reasons for taking a temporary position. For college students who are interested in ~~enter~~ *entering* the workforce, a temporary position can be very beneficial. If young people are concerned about ~~choose~~ *choosing* the wrong profession, career counselors advise them *to* get experience in a variety of fields. They recommend ~~to~~ working in a company on a temporary basis to determine if the job is suitable. Today companies receive hundreds of résumés for one job opening. Therefore, potential workers need to be good at communicating, writing, and problem solving. A temp job allows a person to learn the skills needed to obtain a better position in the future. It may even help to impress potential employers. Companies expect employees to ~~applying~~ apply themselves and sharpen their skills. Job seekers need to show how valuable they are if they want *to* get hired. While working as a temporary employee, workers can prove themselves on the job and let the company ~~to~~ know they are ready for a full-time position.

In **Timed Writing** you will . . .

- practice writing with a time limit.

Practice your test-taking skills with the following practice topic.
Read the prompt. Then follow the steps below.

> Write an essay in which you classify the courses you are
> presently taking or have taken in school. You can categorize
> these in terms of your favorite to least favorite or the most
> appropriate to least appropriate for your future career.

Step 1   **BRAINSTORMING:** 5 minutes

Write down ideas and vocabulary for your essay on a separate piece of paper.

Step 2   **OUTLINING:** 5 minutes

Write an outline for your essay. Use a separate piece of paper if necessary.

Introduction (First Paragraph)	
Hook Capture the reader's attention.	
Background Information Give the reader a broad picture of the issue and why it is important.	
Thesis Statement Clearly explain what is being classified and how it is organized.	
Body Paragraphs (Middle Paragraphs)	
Topics and Controlling Ideas Clearly describe each category or group.	
Supporting Details Include paraphrases, definitions, examples, anecdotes, statistics, or quotations.	
Conclusion (Last Paragraph)	
Restatement of Thesis Include a prediction, advice, or a general statement.	

WRITING: 40 minutes

Use your brainstorming notes and outline to write your essay on a separate piece of paper.

Step 4 **EDITING:** 10 minutes

When you have finished your essay, check it for mistakes using the checklist below.

GO ONLINE

Editor's Checklist

Put a check (✓) as appropriate.

○ 1. Does the introduction tell what is being classified?

○ 2. Does each body paragraph explain a different category?

○ 3. Are the categories arranged according to one unifying principle?

○ 4. Does the conclusion restate the categories?

○ 5. Did you use gerunds correctly?

○ 6. Did you use infinitives correctly?

○ 7. Did you use the correct word pattern for the verbs *make, let,* and *have*?

Go to the Web to print out a peer editor's worksheet.

Topics for Future Writing

Write a classification essay on one of the following topics.

Communications: Types of media: television, Internet, film, newspapers, and books

Environmental Science: Ecosystems: tropics, deserts, rain forests, and savannas

Environmental Technology: Sources of energy: solar, oil, natural gas, thermal, and wind

Geology: Rock formations: igneous, sedimentary, and metamorphic

Health: Food categories: proteins, fats, carbohydrates, and sugars

History: Historical periods in your country

Meteorology: hurricanes, blizzards, tornadoes, and earthquakes

Psychology: Various stages of human development from infancy to old age

Urban Planning: Methods of transportation: boats, cars, buses, planes, and trains

UNIT 6 Reaction Essays

Unit Goals

Critical Thinking Focus
- theme in short stories

Research Focus
- works cited lists

Rhetorical Focus
- reaction organization
- the literary present

Language and Grammar Focus
- passives

A TV commercial has to grasp an audience's attention and get its message across in just a few seconds. Short stories are similar. Short-story writers must build up complex characters, a plot, and a message in just a few pages. In this unit, you will read and respond to the theme, or message, in a short story.

"I love short stories because I believe they are the way we live. They are what our friends tell us, in their pain and joy, their passion and rage, their yearning and their cry against injustice."

—Andre Dubus

"Short stories can be rather stark and bare unless you put in the right details. Details make stories human, and the more human a story can be, the better."

—V.S. Pritchett

Exercise 1 Thinking about the topic

A. Discuss the quotations with a partner.

- According to Andre Dubus, people tell stories about strong emotions. What are some life-changing events that could trigger these emotions?
- V.S. Pritchett emphasizes details in short stories. What are some details that can make a story exciting?

B. Select one of the above quotations and make notes on some of the ideas it presents. Then discuss in small groups.

Short stories not only engage readers, but often make them reflect on their own lives and beliefs. The following reading is a story within a story. What lessons does it teach?

The Shepherd's Daughter

By William Saroyan

It is the opinion of my grandmother that all men should labor, and at the table, a moment ago, she said to me: "You must learn to do some good work, the making of some item useful to man, something out of clay, or out of wood, or metal, or cloth. It is not proper for a young man to be ignorant of an honorable **craft**. Is there anything you can make? Can you make a simple table, a chair, a plain dish, a rug, a coffee pot? Is there anything you can do?"

And my grandmother looked at me with anger.

"I know," she said, "you are supposed to be a writer, and I suppose you are. You certainly smoke enough cigarettes to be anything, and the whole house is full of the smoke, but you must learn to make some solid things, things that can be used, that can be seen and touched."

"There was a king of the Persians," said my grandmother, "and he had a son, and this son fell in love with a shepherd's daughter. He went to his father and he said, 'My Lord, I love a shepherd's daughter, and I would have her for my wife.' And the king said, 'I am king and you are my son, and when I die you shall be king, how can it be that you would marry the daughter of a shepherd?' And the son said, 'My Lord, I do not know, but I know that I love this girl and would have her for my queen.'"

"The king saw that his son's love for the girl was genuine, and he said, 'I will send a message to her.' And he called a messenger to him and he said, 'Go to the shepherd's daughter and say that my son loves her and would have her for his wife.' And the messenger went to the girl and he said, 'The king's son loves you and would have you for his wife.' And the girl said, 'What labor does he do?' And the messenger said, 'Why, he is the son of a king; he does no labor.' And the girl said, 'He must learn to do some labor.' And the messenger returned to the king and spoke the words of the shepherd's daughter."

"The king said to his son, 'The shepherd's daughter wishes you to learn some craft. Would you still have her for your wife?' And the son said, 'Yes, I will learn to weave straw rugs.' And the boy was taught to weave rugs of straw, in patterns and in colors and with **ornamental** designs, and at the end of three days he was making very fine straw rugs, and the messenger returned to the shepherd's daughter, and he said, 'These rugs of straw are the work of the king's son.'"

"And the girl went with the messenger to the king's palace, and she became the wife of the king's son."

"One day," said my grandmother, "the king's son was walking through the streets of Baghdad, and he came upon an eating place which was so clean and cool that he entered it and sat at a table."

"This place," said my grandmother, "was a place of thieves and murderers, and they took the king's son and placed him in a large **dungeon** where many great men of the city were being held, and the thieves and murderers were killing the fattest of the men and feeding them to the **leanest** of them, and **making sport of it**. The king's son was of the leanest of the men, and it was not known that he was the son of the king of the Persians, so his life was spared, and he said to the thieves and murderers, 'I am a weaver of straw rugs, and these rugs have great value.' And they brought him straw and asked him to weave and in three days he weaved three rugs, and he said, 'Carry these to the palace of the king of the Persians, and for each rug he will give you a hundred gold pieces of money.' And the rugs were carried to the palace of the king, and when the king saw the rugs he saw that they were the work of his son, and he took the rugs to the shepherd's daughter and he said, 'These rugs were brought to the palace and they are the work of my son who is lost.' And the shepherd's daughter took each rug and looked at it closely and in the design of each rug she saw in the written language of the Persians a message from her husband, and she related this message to the king."

"And the king," said my grandmother, "sent many soldiers to the place of the thieves and murderers, and the soldiers rescued all the **captives** and killed all the thieves and murderers, and the king's son was returned safely to the palace of his father and to the company of his wife, the little shepherd's daughter. And when the boy went into the palace of his father, and saw again his wife, he **humbled** himself before her and embraced her feet, and he said, 'My love, it is because of you that I am alive,' and the king was greatly pleased with the shepherd's daughter."

"Now," said my grandmother, "do you see why every man should learn an honorable craft?"

"I see very clearly," I said, "and as soon as I earn enough money to buy a saw and a hammer and a piece of **lumber**, I shall do my best to make a simple chair or a shelf for books."

Adapted from Soroyan, William. "The Shepherd's Daughter." *Modern American Short Stories.* Ed. Bennett A. Cerf. Cleveland: Word Publishing, 1945. Print.

craft: an occupation or trade that requires the use of one's hands
ornamental: decorative
dungeon: an underground prison
leanest: thinnest
making sport of it: making fun of
captives: prisoners
humbled: made modest
lumber: wood prepared for building

Exercise 3 Understanding the text

Write *T* for true or *F* for false for each statement.

___T___ 1. According to the grandmother, it is important for young men to make things with their hands.

___F___ 2. The grandmother thinks that writing is an honorable career for a young man.

___T___ 3. The king's son gives the shepherd's daughter credit for saving his life.

___F___ 4. The king's son tricks the thieves by having them make the straw rugs for him.

___T___ 5. The thieves return the prince to the palace because the king buys the rugs for a high price.

Exercise 4 Responding to the text

Respond to the short story by answering the following questions. Compare your answers with a partner.

1. Why does the grandmother tell her grandson the story of the king and his son?

   _____

   _____

   _____

2. What does the shepherd's daughter want the king's son to do before she will agree to marry him?

   _____

   _____

   _____

3. Why don't the thieves kill the king's son?

   _____

   _____

   _____

4. How does the shepherd's daughter know where to find her husband?

   _____

   _____

   _____

5. What lesson does the grandson learn at the end of the story?

   _____

   _____

   _____

Exercise 5 Freewriting

Write for ten to fifteen minutes in your journal. Choose from topics below or an idea of your own. Express your thoughts and feelings. Don't worry about mistakes.

- In the end of "The Shepherd's Daughter" the prince survives because of his weaving skills. What would have happened if he had learned a different skill? Invent a new ending for the story. Does the prince survive?
- Write about a short story you enjoyed reading. What made the story memorable?
- Write about a short story or movie that ended in a surprising way. How did you expect it to end? Would you have preferred a different ending? Why or why not?
- Describe a character you like from a novel, short story, movie, or TV show. What do you like about the character?

 In **Writing Process Step 2** you will . . .

- learn how to analyze the theme of a short story.
- learn about reaction organization.
- brainstorm ideas and specific vocabulary to use in your writing.
- determine the audience and purpose for your reaction essay.
- create an outline for a reaction essay.

WRITING TASK Short-story authors write to entertain their readers. However, these stories often have another purpose. They carry a message that the author wants to give readers. This message is the story's theme. Write an essay for a literary journal in which you react to the theme of a short story. Include quotes and other evidence from the story. Go to the Web to use the Online Writing Tutor.

Exercise 1 Understanding your assignment

Read the writing task again, and answer the following questions. Then discuss your answers with a partner.

1. What is the topic you are asked to write about? _____

2. What story will you react to? _____

3. What publication are you being asked to write for? _____

4. What aspect of the short story will you react to? _____

Critical Thinking Focus

Analyzing Theme

Theme is the message that an author wants to convey to the reader. Often the message is a moral one such as, "There is more to life than money," "Be true to yourself," or "Always stand up for your beliefs."

When you analyze a story's theme, you look for insights the story gives about life. The message is seldom stated directly in the story, so it will take interpretation. Think about the main characters. Do they change? Do they learn anything? Do their experiences reveal a truth about life in general? Do the words in the title suggest any message? Do the words and dialogue among characters state a lesson?

Theme versus Topic

A story's theme is different from its **topic** or **plot**. The topic is what the story is about. It can be stated in a word or two such as, *money, self-worth,* or *justice.* Plots tell what happens in a story. Summarizing a story's plot requires a sentence or more. A story's theme is its message or truth about life. Like the plot, it must be expressed in a sentence or more.

Multiple Themes

Stories often reveal more than one theme. For example, in a single story, an author might give the message, "There is more to life than money" while also conveying the idea, "Money can lead to corruption." Stories are interpreted differently by various readers, so two readers will seldom express a theme in the same words.

Exercise 2 Identifying theme versus topic or plot

For the items below, write *TH* beside each theme. Write *T* beside each topic.
Write *P* beside each plot summary.

   _T_   1. Responsibility

   _TH_ 2. Marriage requires communication.

   _TH_ 3. Power corrupts.

   _T_   4. Childhood friendships

   _TH_ 5. Dreams empower people to achieve.

   _P_   6. She becomes the first woman doctor in her community.

Exercise 3 Brainstorming ideas

A. Use the analysis of the grandmother and grandson's story provided in the chart below as a model for the theme: "What we learn today may have an impact on our future." Then complete an analysis of the story of the king and prince.

CRITERIA	GRANDMOTHER AND GRANDSON	PRINCE AND SHEPHERD'S DAUGHTER
The title	The title says nothing about the theme.	
What characters say	"It is not proper for a young man to be ignorant of an honorable craft."	
How characters change	The grandson decides to make a chair or bookshelf.	
What characters learn	The grandson learns that having a second skill may benefit him.	

B. Complete the chart below with information from a story you have read. Show how the story's title and/or characters reveal the story's theme. Use a separate piece of paper.

CRITERIA	STORY INFORMATION
The title	
What characters say	
How characters change	
What characters learn	

Exercise 4 Considering audience and purpose

Think about your audience and purpose as you answer the questions below.

1. What will your readers need to know about the story to understand your analysis? _____

   _____

   _____

2. Considering the publication you are writing for, what will your audience expect from your reaction? _____

   _____

   _____

3. What do you want your readers to know or learn about the story?

   _____

   _____

   _____

Rhetorical Focus

Reaction Organization

In a **reaction essay** on theme, the writer analyzes and evaluates his or her response to a short story's theme or themes. The writer answers the questions: *What is the story's message? Does the theme relate to life today? What can people learn from this theme?*

Introduction
- The hook grabs the reader's attention. It may make a general comment about the theme. It may be a quotation, an anecdote, or a fact.
- Background information includes the title, author, and perhaps a quick summary of the story.
- The thesis statement tells what theme or themes the writer will react to.

Body Paragraphs
- The topic sentence in each paragraph states one aspect of the story's theme.
- Each paragraph uses examples or quotations from the story to describe a different theme or a different aspect of one theme.

Conclusion
- The conclusion restates the thesis.
- The conclusion summarizes the analysis.
- Conclusions may also evaluate the theme.

Read the essay. What theme does the writer explore?

Valuable Life Lessons

"The best preparation for tomorrow is to do today's work superbly well," advised the Canadian physician William Osler. This valuable message is also interwoven into William Saroyan's short story "The Shepherd's Daughter." The story focuses on a grandmother who is deeply concerned about her grandson's future. Saroyan weaves two stories together to convey the idea that it is important to prepare for the future.

"The Shepherd's Daughter" begins with a grandmother encouraging her grandson to develop a practical skill. Although the grandson is an aspiring writer, his grandmother worries that he will not be able to support himself in his career. While advising her grandson, she insists, "You must learn to do some good work, the making of some item useful to man, something out of clay, or out of wood, or metal, or cloth." She uses a story about a prince and a shepherd's daughter to persuade her grandson to pursue a more productive profession.

As students, we know that what we learn today impacts our future lives. The prince in "The Shepherd's Daughter" is not aware of this fact. When he decides to learn how to weave rugs, his initial goal is only to satisfy his future wife's request. However, he does much more than just learn to weave rugs. He designs magnificent and colorful patterns that are considered superb. It is not until he faces a life-threatening situation that he discovers the true value of his work. He uses the straw rugs to communicate with his family. With their help, he is rescued from thieves and murderers.

After hearing the story about the prince, the grandson agrees to develop a practical skill. He decides to build either a chair or a shelf for his books. Thus, he combines his love for writing with another skill that can be used in the future. With skills in woodworking, he can build a comfortable chair to sit in as he writes. If he becomes a successful writer, well-built bookshelves will provide an excellent place to display his published books. On the other hand, if he is not successful at writing, he can fall back on his woodworking skills.

"The Shepherd's Daughter" is an exciting short story with a powerful theme. It reveals the importance of carefully considering future career options and planning alternatives. Perhaps we should all consider other options, just in case we do not succeed at our chosen professions.

Works Cited

Saroyan, William. "The Shepherd's Daughter." Modern American Short Stories. ed. Bennett A. Cerf. Cleveland: Word Publishing, 1945. Print.

Exercise 6 Examining the student essay

A. Respond to the essay by answering the following questions.

1. What theme is the student writer analyzing in the essay?

   _____

   _____

2. What evidence does the student writer give that the prince doesn't think learning a craft will benefit him personally?

   _____

   _____

3. According to the student writer, how will skills in woodworking benefit the grandson?

   _____

   _____

4. How does the student writer relate the theme to life today?

   _____

   _____

B. Examine the organization of the essay by responding to the questions below. Then compare your answers with a partner.

1. How does the quote in the hook relate to the essay's thesis?

    _____

    _____

2. What does the essay's title reveal about the student writer's opinion of the story's theme?

    _____

    _____

3. In body paragraph 1, the student writer includes a quotation from the short story. How does the quotation help explain the grandmother's position?

    _____

    _____

4. In body paragraph 2, how does the student writer use evidence from the story to support the idea that what we learn now impacts our future lives?

    _____

    _____

5. What advice does the writer give in his conclusion?

    _____

    _____

Exercise 7 Writing an outline

GO ONLINE

Review your brainstorming ideas and your freewriting exercise. Then go to the Web to print out an outline template for your essay.

 In **Writing Process Step 3** you will . . .

- learn to use the literary present.
- learn how to write Works Cited lists.
- write a first draft of your reaction essay.

Exercise 1 Reading a student essay

Read the essay. What themes does the writer explore?

The Value of Work

The French author George Sand once wrote, "Work is not man's punishment. It is his reward and his strength and his pleasure." This certainly mirrors the ideas of William Saroyan's short story "The Shepherd's Daughter." Multiple themes play out in this tale, perhaps due to the fact that the work contains two stories. The themes of each story are similar. They both express the need for having skills; however, the story of the prince and the shepherd's daughter also brings to mind the concept that social status is not enough to make a person truly worthy.

The story begins with a grandmother admonishing her grandson. She complains that, "It is not proper for a young man to be ignorant of an honorable craft." The young man's chosen career as a writer is not taken seriously by the grandmother. Through a short story, the grandmother warns her grandson that he must learn to make something with his hands.

The grandmother teaches her lesson through a short story about a prince who has fallen in love with a shepherd's daughter and requests her hand in marriage. The story suggests that the prince has inherited his position and has never learned how to do or make anything useful. The shepherd's daughter responds to the prince's proposal with, "He must learn to do some labor." Like the grandmother, she places great importance on a person's skill.

This leads to a confrontation between different value systems, that of the rich and that of the poor. The prince in the story is privileged and has inherited a title that gives him great power over others. As king, he will rule, but what are his qualifications for the job? The shepherd's daughter is poor. She knows the value of hard, honest work. She probably did not receive formal schooling, but in this story it is the shepherd's daughter who is wise. She understands what survival means and wants to be sure her future husband has the discipline to learn something practical. Of the two lifestyles—one supported by inherited wealth and the other by hard work—it is the shepherd's daughter whose determination helps save the day.

While the story of the prince and the shepherd's daughter is understood to be old, it carries themes that are universal over time and distance. The message is understood well into the twentieth century when the grandmother tells the story. The grandson understands the message and concedes that he will learn woodworking. However, he says this with a bit of caution. He will not give up his writing, but instead put his woodworking skills to use in building a chair for his writing desk or a bookcase for his books.

Saroyan's short story seamlessly weaves together several important lessons. The stories reveal the value of hard work. Saroyan also conveys the message that one doesn't have to have money to be smart and understand the importance of a job well done. These messages are as true today as they were during the Middle Ages and the twentieth century when the story was written.

Exercise 2 Examining a student essay

A. Respond to the essay by answering the following questions.

1. How does the writer interpret the grandmother's attitude toward her grandson's profession?

   _____

   _____

2. What does the writer believe about the relationship between status and intelligence?

   _____

   _____

3. What do the shepherd's daughter and the grandmother have in common?

   _____

   _____

4. What is the writer's opinion of differences in social classes?

   _____

   _____

B. Examine the organization of the essay by responding to the questions below. Compare your answers with a partner.

1. What does the writer use to engage her readers in the introduction?

   _____

   _____

2. What information does the writer give in the background?

   _____

   _____

3. Reread the thesis statement. What two themes does the writer explore?

   _____

   _____

4. How does the writer use quotations and evidence from the story to support her ideas?

   _____

   _____

5. What is the writer's opinion of the story's themes? How do you know?

   _____

   _____

Rhetorical Focus

The Literary Present

Short stories are often written in the simple past as if they were reporting events from the past. When writers react to literature; however, they use the **simple present**. This is called *the literary present*.

The Simple Past in "The Shepherd's Daughter"

"There **was** a king of the Persians," **said** my grandmother, "and he **had** a son, and this son **fell** in love with a shepherd's daughter. He **went** to his father and he **said** . . .

The Literary Present in the Reaction Essay

The grandmother **teaches** her lesson through a short story about a prince who **has fallen** in love with a shepherd's daughter and **requests** her hand in marriage. The story **suggests** that the prince **has inherited** his position and **has** never **learned** to do or make anything useful.

A. Use the literary present to complete each of the sentences below.

1. The grandmother in Saroyan's story <u>is concerned about her grandson's</u> <u>future.</u>

2. At the beginning of the story, the grandson _doesn't care about_ _his grandmom._

3. Because of the prince's new skill, he ~~servives~~. Surviv**es**

4. After hearing the story, the grandson _understands the story._

5. The theme of the story ~~is talking~~ talks _about people should learn more skill in case they fail one skill._

B. Use the literary present tense to write sentences for your essay.

Grandmother is concerned about her grandson's future. At the beginning of the story, the grandson doesn't care about her.

Research Focus

Works Cited Lists

When you use other people's ideas in a researched essay, you must cite your sources within the essay. In some cases you might want to provide full citations at the end of the essay to show your readers just where to go to find the original sources. Developing a Works Cited list is a good way to show all the sources you use.

When you develop a Works Cited list, you organize your sources in alphabetical order according to each author's last name. However, different types of entries in your list require different formats, so be careful to write out your citations correctly.

See Appendix II in this book for more on writing Works Cited lists.

1. Book

The information for the citation should be taken from the book's title page.

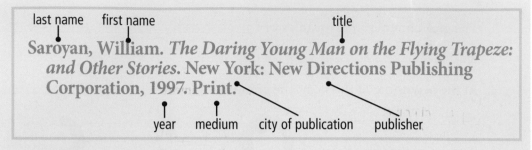

2. Story in an Anthology

An anthology is a collection of literary works, such as poems, essays, or short stories. Most anthologies are compiled by editors.

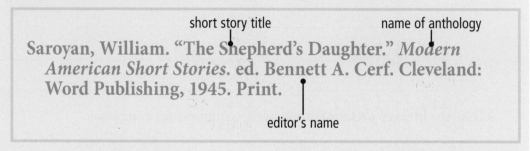

3. Article in a Newspaper

For a newspaper article, the title of the article is placed in quotation marks with initial capital letters. The title of the publication is in italics.

4. Article on a Website

When you cite an Internet source, give the date that you accessed the site as well as the day the content was posted. You do not have to provide the URL.

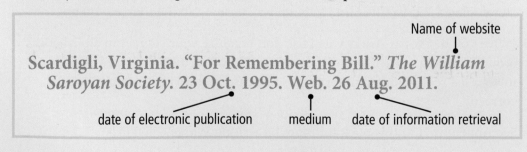

Exercise 4 Creating a Works Cited list

A. Write Works Cited entries from the information in the items below. Use a separate piece of paper.

1	Name of Website:	Literary Traveler
	Article Title:	Fernando Pessoa's Lisbon of Disquiet
	Article Author:	Stephen Hermans
	Date of Article:	June 1, 2010
	Date of Retrieval:	November 20, 2012
	Medium:	Website

2	Name of Anthology:	50 Great Short Stories
	Story Title:	The Other Two
	Story Author:	Edith Wharton
	Year of Publication:	2005
	City of Publication:	New York
	Medium:	Print
	Publisher:	Bantam Dell
	Editor:	Milton Crane

3	Name of Newspaper:	The Capital Times
	Article Title:	Short Stories Harvest Emotional Landscapes
	Article Author:	Rob Thomas
	Date of Article:	August 25, 2006
	Medium:	Print

B. Write the number of each above citation on the line in the appropriate order for a Works Cited list.

3
1
2

Exercise 5 Writing a first draft

GO ONLINE

Review your outline. Then write the first draft of a reaction essay. Go to the Web to use the Online Writing Tutor.

Exercise 6 Peer editing a first draft

GO ONLINE

A. After writing a first draft, it is helpful to get feedback on your ideas. Exchange essays with two other people. For each essay you read, answer the Peer Editor's Questions on a separate piece of paper. Then discuss your responses.

Peer Editor's Questions

1. What short story is the writer reacting to?

2. What theme in the story is the writer reacting to?

3. What information does the writer give about the story to help you understand its theme?

4. What do you like best about the essay?

5. What advice can you give to the writer to improve the essay?

Go to the Web to print out a peer editor's worksheet.

B. Review your feedback and the organization guidelines on page 186. Make notes for your revision. In this step, you may add, remove, or rewrite information to clarify your ideas.

 In **Writing Process Step 4** you will . . .

- learn about passives.
- learn about passives without an agent.
- learn about verbs with no passive forms.
- edit your first draft and write a final draft.

Now that you have written a first draft, it is time to edit. Editing involves making changes to your writing to improve it and to correct mistakes.

Language and Grammar Focus

GO ONLINE

Passives

Writers use **passive** sentences in reaction essays when they want to emphasize a person or thing that does not perform an action but instead receives the action.

To form the passive, use *BE* and a **past participle**. The person or thing that performs the task is called the *agent*. Passive verb forms are often followed by the preposition *by* plus the **agent**.

| BE + past participle | | agent |

The prince **is rescued** by **the king's soldiers**.

Passive sentences change the order of the subject and object of an **active sentence**.

The subject of an active sentence then becomes the agent.

Active Sentence: The king's soldiers rescue the prince.
Passive Sentence: The prince is rescued by the king's soldiers.

The object of an active sentence becomes the subject of the passive sentence.

Active

| subject | | object |

Students all over the world read   the stories of Anton Chekhov.

Passive

| subject | | agent |

The stories of Anton Chekhov are read by students all over the world.

The passive form is used in all the tenses.

Active (simple past)

Anton Chekhov wrote "Uncle Vanya."

Passive (past)

"Uncle Vanya" was written by Anton Chekhov.

Active (future with *will*)

The theater department will perform Ibsen's "A Doll's House."

Passive (future with *will*)

Ibsen's "A Doll's House" will be performed by the theater department.

Exercise 1 Changing active sentences to passive

Rewrite the active sentences below as passive sentences.

1. Animated films fascinate most young children.

   Most young children are fascinated by animated films.

2. A solo voice with a choir performed this piece of music.

   This piece of music was performed by a solo voice with a choir.

3. The capture of the prince heightens the suspense of the story.

   The suspense of the story is heightened by the capture of the prince.

4. The prince sent the straw rugs to save his life.

5. The thieves captured the prince while he was sitting at a table.

Language and Grammar Focus

Passives without an Agent

In many passive sentences the agent can be omitted. Here are a few reasons to omit the agent.

- The agent is obvious or not important.

  The story is set in Rome.

- The agent is not known.

  A priceless artwork was stolen from the Prado yesterday.

- The writer wants to avoid saying who is responsible for an action or event.

  The news story was leaked to the press over the weekend.

- The agent is a general noun (a person, people) or a pronoun (*someone, we, one, you,* or *they*).

  Crops are harvested in the autumn.

> **!** Be sure to use an agent when it is important to know who performed a particular action.
>
> *Romeo and Juliet* was written by Shakespeare.

Exercise 2 Omitting agents with passives

Change the following sentences from active to passive. Do not include the agent.

1. The booking agent might cancel the outdoor concert due to rain.

   The outdoor concert might be canceled due to rain.

2. Parents should not allow children to watch television all day.

   Children should not be allowed to watch TV all days.

3. Individuals can read books on hand-held devices.

   Books on Hand-held devices can be read.

4. People should not quote an author without giving the source.

   An author [without giving the source] shouldn't be quoted.

5. A person can read a short story out loud for more enjoyment.

   A short story can be read out loud for more enjoyment

6. The publishers will extend the deadline until the end of the summer.

   The deadline until the end of the summer will be extended

Exercise 3 Including or omitting agents with passives

Change the following active sentences to passive. Omit the agent when it is not necessary.

1. The reviewer rewrote the story before final publication.

   The story was rewritten before final publication.

2. Their desire to graduate on time motivates many students.

   _____

3. People consider Edgar Allan Poe the father of the short story.

   _____

4. Readers remember some writers for their exquisite language.

   _____

5. In a film, the music can create many different moods.

   _____

Verbs with No Passive Forms

Intransitive verbs are not followed by an object and do not have a passive form. Common intransitive verbs include:

arrive	be	become
come	disagree	fall
go	happen	look
recover	run	sit
sleep	stand	struggle

Some **transitive verbs** also do not have passive forms. These include:

become	cost	fit	have	resemble

Exercise 4 Recognizing verbs with no passive forms

Change the sentences to the passive form. If the verb in the sentence does not have a passive form, write _X_ next to the sentence.

_____ 1. The grandmother disagreed with the way her grandson was living.

_____

_____

_____ 2. A student can find books by Shakespeare in most college libraries.

_____

_____

_____ 3. The designer built the set for a small stage.

_____

_____

_____ 4. The short story became popular in the mid-nineteenth century.

_____

_____

_____ 5. The characters in a novel often resemble real people in the author's life.

_____

_____

Exercise 5 Editing paragraphs

Read the paragraphs. Correct the mistakes in passive structure. There are six more mistakes.

                                             written
        "The Happy Man's Shirt" was ~~write~~ by the Italian author Italo Calvino. The story conveys the idea that true happiness is often misunderstand, can be difficult to recognize, and is not easily to find. The story is about a king who is deeply concerned and worried about his son. The prince, it seems, suffers from a form of acute depression, but no one has any idea what is causing the condition. The king decides to take action. All his wise men are gather together to find a solution to the problem, and after much deliberation, they decide that the problem can be solved. The king and his advisors decide that they must find a truly happy man who is content with his life and wants nothing more. When this man is found, he must wear the prince's shirt. The prince, in turn, must wear the shirt of the happy man.

        Thus the quest begins. There are many close calls, for it becomes evident that finding a truly happy person is no small task. Finally, a young man heard singing the most enchanting and beautiful song imaginable. The young man's song suggests that he is truly happy, so the king believes that he has accomplished his goal. After the young man is asking the necessary questions to determine if he is, in fact, a truly happy man, the king is overjoyed. He now believes that his son will to be saved. However, as he goes to look under the jacket of the young man, he discovers that the young man has no shirt on at all. The happy man is too poor to afford a shirt. Perhaps his happiness stems from the fact that the man is unencumbered by possessions. Instead, he is able to find happiness in simplicity.

Exercise 6 Editing your first draft and rewriting

Review your essay for content, organization, and language mistakes. Use the checklist below. Then write a final draft. Go to the Web to use the Online Writing Tutor.

GO ONLINE

Editor's Checklist

Put a check (✓) as appropriate.

CONTENT AND ORGANIZATION

○ 1. Does your hook relate well to the story's theme?

○ 2. Do you provide enough information to help your readers understand what happened in the story?

○ 3. Does your thesis statement tell readers what theme you will react to?

○ 4. Do your body paragraphs provide evidence and quotations from the story to support your analysis of the theme?

○ 5. Does your conclusion include your reaction to the theme and its importance to life in general?

LANGUAGE

○ 6. Did you use the literary present?

○ 7. Did you use passives? Can they be made into active sentences, or are your ideas clearer in the passive?

○ 8. If you used passives, did you use them correctly?

Go to the Web to print out a peer editor's worksheet.

 In **Review** you will . . .

- review using the literary present.
- practice citing sources.
- review the use of passives.

In Putting It All Together you will review the concepts you learned in this unit.

Exercise 1 Using the literary present

Write about the following story's theme using the literary present.

> ### The Fisherman and His Flute
> by Aesop
>
> A fisherman skilled in music took his flute and his nets to the seashore. After he cast his net into the sea, he played several tunes. He hoped the fish would dance their way into his net.
>
> He waited a long while, but no fish arrived. Finally, he laid his flute aside. Suddenly, a school of fish leaped about in his net.

_____

_____

_____

_____

_____

Exercise 2 Creating a works cited list

Write a Works Cited entry for a book and a website article you have read recently.

BOOK

WEBSITE

Exercise 3 Changing active sentences to the passive

Rewrite the active sentences below as passive sentences.

1. Readers around the world appreciate great works of fiction. _____
   _____

2. Students studying comparative literature can buy used books online. _____
   _____

3. Publishing companies often sponsor international book fairs. _____
   _____

4. Graduate students must include a Works Cited list at the end of their dissertations.
   _____

5. Oxford University Press published this book. _____
   _____

Exercise 4 Using passives with and without agents

**Rewrite the active sentences below as passive sentences. Omit the agent when it
is not necessary.**

1. The principal must approve the changes to the schedule. _____
   _____

2. People must charge cell phones on a regular basis. _____
   _____

3. People don't usually close theaters on national holidays. _____
   _____

4. In Korea, people grow soybeans, wheat, and cucumbers. _____
   _____

5. The *International Herald Tribune* publishes a weekend edition. _____
   _____

Exercise 5 Editing a paragraph

Read the paragraph and edit as necessary. There are eight mistakes.

What happens to someone who is suddenly given an unexpected gift? If a person is frugal like the character Mrs. Sommers in Kate Chopin's short story "A Pair of Silk Stockings," she might have good intentions but be led astray. Mrs. Sommers found $15 and is driven by her desire to spend it carefully. Due to her modest circumstances, she must always look for a bargain, so she starts with a list of practical items she feels she should buy. However, she slowly lured into a series of temptations she cannot resist. The most important of these was a pair of incredibly soft and luxurious silk stockings. These items would never before be allow on her tight budget. As readers we are taken into her world of desires. She overwhelms by the soft touch of these stockings. Even better, the price has been reduced. She feels that she is almost forced to buy them. From there it is an easy journey to spending more, moving from stockings to shoes to gloves to high-priced magazines. The choices now seemed endless. Interestingly her personality is even change as she joins the crowds feeling more self-assured. She eats a sumptuous meal in a restaurant she had only admired but never dared to enter before. She ended her day at the theater where she is captivated by the comedy. At the end we feel she has deserved this day and, like her, we wish it could go on forever.

 In **Timed Writing** you will . . .

- practice writing with a time limit.

Practice your test-taking skills. Read the short story. Then follow the steps to write a reaction to a theme in the story.

The Ninny

By Anton Chekhov

Just a few days ago I invited Yulia Vassilyevna, the governess of my children, to come to my study. I wanted to settle my account with her.

"Sit down, Yulia Vassilyevna," I said to her. "Let's get our accounts settled. I'm sure you need some money, but you keep standing on ceremony and never ask for it. Let me see. We agreed to give you thirty rubles a month, didn't we?"

"Forty."

"No, thirty. I made a note of it. I always pay the governess thirty. Now, let me see. You have been with us for two months?"

"Two months and five days."

"Two months exactly. I made a note of it. So you have sixty rubles coming to you. Subtract nine Sundays. You know you don't tutor Kolya on Sundays, you just go out for a walk. And then the three holidays. . . ."

Yulia Vassilyevna blushed and picked at the trimmings of her dress, but didn't say a word.

"Three holidays. So we take off twelve rubles. Kolya was sick for four days—those days you didn't look after him. You looked after Vanya, only Vanya. Then there were the three days you had a toothache, when my wife gave you permission to take a break from the children after dinner. Twelve and seven makes nineteen. Subtract . . . That leaves . . . hm . . . forty-one rubles. Correct?"

Yulia Vassilyevna's left eye reddened and filled with tears. Her chin trembled. She began to cough nervously, blew her nose and said nothing.

"Then around New Year's Day you broke a cup and saucer. Subtract two rubles. The cup cost more than that—it was an heirloom, but we won't bother about that. We're the ones who pay. And there's another matter. Due to your carelessness Kolya climbed a tree and tore his coat. Subtract ten. Also, due to your carelessness, the chambermaid ran off with Varya's boots. You ought to have kept your eyes open. You get a good salary. So we take off five more . . . On the tenth of January you took ten rubles from me."

"I didn't," Yulia Vassilyevna whispered.

"But I made a note of it."

"Well, yes—perhaps . . ."

"From forty-one we take twenty-seven. That leaves fourteen."

Her eyes filled with tears and her thin, pretty little nose was shining with perspiration. Poor girl!

"I only took money once," she said in a trembling voice. "I took three rubles from your wife . . . never anything more."

"Did you really? You see, I never made a note of it. Take three from fourteen. That leaves eleven. Here's your money, my dear. Three, three, three . . . one and one. Take it, my dear."

I gave her the eleven rubles. With trembling fingers she took them and slipped them into her pocket.

"*Merci,*" she whispered.

I jumped up, and began pacing up and down the room. I was in a furious temper.

"Why did you say '*merci*'?" I asked.

"For the money."

"Don't you realize I've been cheating you? I steal your money and all you can say is '*merci*'!"

"In my other places they gave me nothing."

"They gave you nothing! Well, no wonder! I was playing a trick on you—a dirty trick . . . I'll give you your eighty rubles; they are all here in an envelope made out for you. Is it possible for anyone to be such a nitwit? Why didn't you protest? Why did you keep your mouth shut? Is it possible that there is anyone in this world who is so spineless? Why are you such a ninny?

She gave me a bitter little smile. On her face I read the words: "Yes, it is possible."

I apologized for having played this cruel trick on her, and to her great surprise, I gave her the eighty rubles. And then she said, "*merci*" again several times, always timidly, and went out. I gazed after her, thinking how very easy it is in this world to take advantage of the weak.

———

Chekhov, Anton. "The Ninny." *The Image of Chekhov: Forty Stories by Anton Chekhov in the Order in Which They Were Written.* New York: Alfred Knoff, 1963. Print.

Step 1   BRAINSTORMING: 5 minutes

Write down ideas and vocabulary for your essay. Use the following chart.

CRITERIA	STORY TITLE: "THE NINNY"
The title	
What characters say	
How characters change	
What characters learn	

Test-Taking Tip

Remember to relate the theme of the story to the world at large.

OUTLINING: 5 minutes

Write an outline for your essay.

Introduction (First Paragraph)	
Hook Capture the reader's attention by focusing on a unique aspect of the short story.	
Background Information Identify the title of the story, author, and any other general information.	
Thesis Statement Name the theme that you will react to.	
Body Paragraphs (Middle Paragraphs)	
Topics and Controlling Ideas Analyze how the story reveals its theme.	
Supporting Details Provide evidence from the story to support your ideas.	
Conclusion (Last Paragraph)	
Thesis Restatement and Comment Restate the thesis, and provide an evaluation or comment about how the story's theme relates to life in general.	

Step 3   WRITING: 40 minutes

Use your brainstorming notes and outline to write your essay on a separate piece of paper.

Step 4   EDITING: 10 minutes

When you have finished your essay, check it for mistakes using the checklist below.

GO ONLINE

Editor's Checklist

Put a check (✓) as appropriate.

- ○ 1. Does the essay provide enough background information for your readers to understand the short story?
- ○ 2. Is there a thesis statement that focuses the essay?
- ○ 3. Does the essay explain the short story's theme?
- ○ 4. Do the paragraphs analyze the theme with significant evidence from the story?
- ○ 5. Did you use the literary present?
- ○ 6. Did you use passives correctly?
- ○ 7. Does the conclusion reveal your opinion of the story's theme?

Go to the Web to print out a peer editor's worksheet.

Topics for Future Writing

Write a reaction essay on one of the following topics.

History: React to a quote by a famous historical personality. For example, you might use this one by Mohandas Gandhi: "A 'No' uttered from the deepest conviction is better than a 'Yes' merely uttered to please, or worse, to avoid trouble."

Law: React to a new law or policy being implemented in your state or country. Who will the law or policy affect? How will it change lives?

Media Studies: React to a news report. Discuss its historical context, how well it was reported, and any lessons that can be drawn from the reported event.

Political Science: React to a theme in a speech by a well-known political figure. Tell how you feel about it, if you agree or disagree with its message, and/or how you relate to its content.

Theater Arts: React to a theme of a play you have seen or read.

Appendices

Step 1: Stimulating Ideas

1. **Choose a topic** that interests you and that you would like to know more about. Remember you will be spending a lot of time on this project, and you will want to stay engaged and enjoy the process. If you have been assigned a topic, try to find an angle that interests you. Briefly freewrite on the topic to see what you already know and what observations you can make.

2. **Get an overview** of your topic. Encyclopedias, either in print or online, can give you a basic idea of the scope of your topic. The encyclopedia can act as a reliable reference when you later look at websites. You might read a short essay or watch a documentary about the topic to give you a better idea of where to start. Take notes, listing main points for your research. Develop some questions that you will want to explore.

Step 2: Brainstorming and Outlining

1. **Focus your topic.** Once you have formulated a general topic, you need to evaluate it. If the topic is too broad, you could have too much information. To demonstrate your grasp of the subject, the topic has to be manageable. You will have to narrow it. For example, if the topic is Technology's Influence on Society, you could narrow the topic by developing some initial questions, such as:

   • How has the medical field improved with recent technological advances?

   • How has human interaction changed because of computer technologies?

   • How have technological advances affected employment in the last decade?

   • How have families been affected by the Internet?

   On the other hand, if the topic is too narrow, you won't be able to find enough to say. In this case, you will have to broaden the topic.

2. **Research your topic.**

   • **Make a list of keywords** associated with your topic. These will often be words you encountered in your overview of the topic. Use these words for your Internet search. If your topic is Computer Technology's Influence on Human Interaction, the following keywords may be useful: *technology, human interaction, social media, email, text messaging, chat, Web 2.0, virtual community, social networking, blogs, social commerce, wiki, video games.*

- **Develop your preliminary thesis statement.** After conducting some research, you can develop a preliminary thesis statement. In this statement, you will take a position on a topic.
  - The thesis needs to be specific, focused, and concise.
  - It should capture your readers' attention.
- **Conduct further research.** To deepen your knowledge of the topic, explore the following sources:
  - **Traditional sources** such as books, academic journals, autobiographies, magazines, reference books, and newspapers. Remember to scan bibliographies of relevant books and periodicals to find other sources that might be valuable and relevant to your topic.
  - **Electronic sources** such as electronic databases, ebooks, PDF documents, Web pages, broadcasts, and other multimedia. Most colleges have extensive electronic databases on their library websites.
  - **Primary sources** such as interviews, emails, surveys, questionnaires, letters, diaries, and personal observations.
- **Record your research findings and sources.** Use index cards, a notebook, or a document created online to keep records of your sources. Identify the books, websites, articles, and media from which you have taken your material. Include all information you will need to find the source again and to cite it in your Works Cited List. (See **Appendix II.**)
- **Annotate your research. Summarize, evaluate, and reflect on each source.**
  1. **Summarize** what you have read. In your own words, write down the main points that the author has made.
  2. **Evaluate** the material and decide whether it is trustworthy. Ask yourself the following questions:
     - Is it reliable? Does the information presented confirm what I have already found?
     - Do the ideas seem slanted to one particular point of view, or are they balanced?
     - Who is the author, and what are his or her credentials?
     - Is the information up-to-date so that the statistics and facts are still valid?
     - Does the argument sound too extreme or too simplistic?
     - Does the information come from a reputable organization such as a university or a government agency?

Does the Internet make people more or less social?

Summary: A study by Stanford University indicates that people who use the Internet five or more hours a week spend less time interacting with other people.

Evaluation: The study was by a respectable university, but the article is from Feb. 2000, so it is pretty old. This was before social networking became popular.

Reflection: I think this study is outdated. People use the Internet in a much more social way now.

Source: Margulies, Jonathan. "Internet May Cut Down on Human Interaction." *The Daily Pennsylvanian.* 17 Feb. 2000. Web. 12 Dec. 2012. http://www.dailypennsylvanian.com/node/19497

3. Reflect on what you have read. Is the information relevant to your argument? Has it changed your opinion about your topic? If so, you might want to revise your thesis statement.

3. **Create an outline.**

Outlines help writers to plan their writing systematically. In some cases, instructors require outlines so that they can provide feedback during the writing process. **Outlines help writers to:**

- remain focused on the topic.

- organize headings and subheadings.

- logically order the material.

- evaluate how much material has been collected to support the thesis.

- manage large amounts of information.

- understand relationships among ideas.

Thesis Statement: The Internet has led to human interaction on a scale that was unthinkable in the past.

I. Starting with sharing of information on web sites and through chats and email, humans began to communicate in new ways in the 1990s.

    a. People who had no way to publish their work could post their ideas to the Web.

    b. People began to chat with each other in real time over chat lines.

    c. Email allowed people to share letters as well as documents without having to wait for the postal service.

II. Social networking allows people to reconnect with people they had lost contact with.

    a. People can post résumés and reconnect with past colleagues.

    b. People can share photographs with family members in other countries.

    c. People can post comments and get feedback quickly from friends around the world.

Step 3: Developing Your Ideas

After you have completed your outline, you can begin to write the introduction and body paragraphs. Each of the subtopics will become the topic sentence of the body paragraph. Include researched information from your notes and cite all sources. (See Appendix II: Citing Sources.)

1. **Introductory paragraphs** set the tone of the essay or report. The introduction can have more than one paragraph. The thesis statement should appear toward the end of the introductory paragraphs, but it is not necessarily the last sentence. The introduction may begin with a hook. The introduction should:
   • generalize the theme to connect to the audience and show the importance of the topic.
   • give background information that creates a context for the reader.

2. **Body paragraphs should:**
   • begin with topic sentences, which are generally taken from the main headings of the outline.
   • move from the general to the specific.
   • include evidence from your notes, such as quotations, paraphrases, statistics, and other findings.
   • conclude with clear connections to the thesis statement.

3. **Conclusion.** All of your effort is validated in the conclusion. Here you will summarize your key points and make your final observations. You must:
   • restate your thesis.
   • evaluate and analyze your main ideas.
   • consider the significance and consequences of your findings.

4. **Formatting research reports according to MLA Style**
   Title Page. When writing a research report in Modern Language Association (MLA) style, it is not necessary to include a separate title page. The information is included on the first page of the essay or report. It should be justified to the left, placed at the top of the page, and double-spaced. Use the following order:
   • the writer's name
   • the instructor's name
   • the course name and number
   • the date

Double-space and center the title, which should be in initial capital letters but not in italics, underlined, or placed in quotation marks.

Hassan Mansour

Professor V. Yassi

English 101

December 15, 2012

The Internet's Influence on Human Interaction

In Yemen, a man watches as his granddaughter folds an origami crane in Japan. The two have never met in person, but they use their computers to see each other and talk every week. When people first spent long hours on the Internet, sociologists were afraid people would lose social skills. Instead, they have developed new ones. The Internet has led to human interaction on a scale that was unthinkable in the past.

Parenthetical Citations are used to identify the source of your researched data. These may be quotations, paraphrases, or summaries. Refer to Appendix II: Citing Sources.

Works Cited is an alphabetical list of sources used in your research. It includes the authors, names, titles, publication information, and dates. It is formatted in MLA style. Refer to the Works Cited section of Appendix II: Citing Sources.

Step 4: Editing Your Writing

1. **Revising.** Revision is often an underestimated process, but no essay or report is complete without it. Before revising, set your writing aside for a day or so. When you return to it, you can read your work again with a fresh outlook. Reflect, rethink, refine your goals, and reconsider your choices. Polish your details and eliminate information that does not support your thesis. Read your work out loud to make sure there is a natural flow. Check that:

   - your thesis statement is still strong and takes a clear position.
   - you have not stated something obvious or too vague.
   - your information is accurate.
   - the introduction and conclusion are engaging and insightful.
   - details in the body paragraphs support the thesis.
   - there is a logical flow of ideas and the organization makes sense.
   - there are appropriate transitions within and between paragraphs to connect your ideas.

2. **Editing** is proofreading for grammar, spelling, vocabulary, and mechanics. If you keep track of your errors, you can distinguish patterns and avoid repeating them. Here are some guidelines.

- Review vocabulary. If you have repeated the same words, use a dictionary and a thesaurus to find synonyms.
- Try to incorporate academic words.
- Check spelling and word usage. The spell-check and grammar-check on a computer are often not accurate and will not detect misused words.
- Correct any sentence fragments, run-on sentences, or comma splices.
- Check punctuation.
- Check correct use of MLA style for parenthetical citations and Works Cited entries.

When you write researched essays, your instructor might want you to cite your sources according to a specific style such as MLA. If so, follow the rules in this appendix. Researched essays do not always require such strict citations, but research reports do. If your assignment is to write a report rather than an essay, check with your instructor to determine if you will use MLA or another style to format your report. The information in this book will apply only if you are using MLA style.

Using Parenthetical Citations within the Text

Parenthetical citations identify where your research is from. Use parenthetical citations when you quote, paraphrase, or summarize outside sources.

Rules for citations within the text:

Cite both the author's name and the page number where you found the information.
> "I have experimented with many forms of exercise in my life, and I keep coming back to walking as the best" (Weil 190).

Set the citation in parentheses.
> (Gladwell 239)

Place the citation at the end of the quotation, summary, or paraphrase.
> "If you want to succeed, you must work hard" (Gladwell 239).

Place final punctuation after the citation.
> "If you want to succeed, you must work hard" (Gladwell 239).

If the author's name is mentioned in the essay or report, provide only the page number(s).
> As Malcolm Gladwell says in his popular book *Outliers,* "Working really hard is what successful people do" (239).

If there are three or more authors, list only the first author's last name followed by et al. and the page number.
> "Life inevitably offers a mixture of good and bad times, triumphs and defeats, periods of bliss and periods of sadness, loss or even humiliation" (Liberman et al. 606).

Works Cited

At the end of your research report you will need a Works Cited list. This list gives all the references used in alphabetical order according to the author's last name.

Different types of entries in your list require different formats, so be careful to write out your citation correctly. The following are examples of how to format entries from different sources.

Books

The information for the citation should be taken from the book's title page.

1. One Author

2. Two or Three Authors

Note that only the first author's name is reversed.

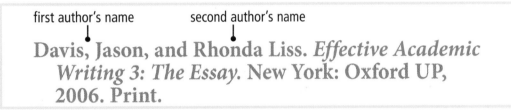

3. More than Three Authors

Note that only the first author's name is mentioned followed by *et al.*

4. Editor(s)

In some instances no author exists for a book. Instead, there are editors. If only one editor is mentioned, follow the name with *ed.* If more are listed, use *eds.*

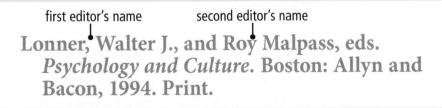

5. Newspaper Article

The title of the article is placed in quotation marks with initial capital letters, and the title of the publication is in italics.

article title

Galeano, Eduardo. "Messi Is Barcelona's Boy Genius." *New York Times* 22 May 2011: N1. Print.

title of newspaper   date   section and page number

6. Magazine Article

Patterson, Jim. "Embracing Small Wind." *E-The Environmental Magazine* Nov.–Dec. 2010: 34. Print.

title of magazine   date   page number

7. Academic Journal

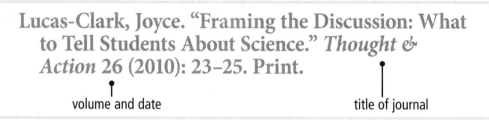

Lucas-Clark, Joyce. "Framing the Discussion: What to Tell Students About Science." *Thought & Action* 26 (2010): 23–25. Print.

volume and date   title of journal

8. Review of One Work

last name of the reviewer   first name of the reviewer   title of review

Laird, Nick. "The Triumph of Paul Muldoon." Rev. of *Maggot,* by Paul Muldoon. *The New York Review of Books* 23 June 2011: 63–66. Print.

title and author of book reviewed

9. Review of Multiple Works

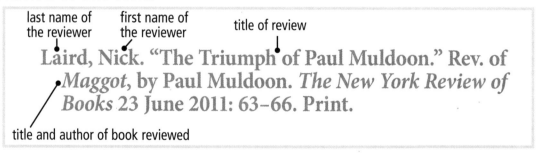

titles and authors of books reviewed

Halpern, Sue. "Mind Control & the Internet." Rev. of *World Wide Mind: The Coming Integration of Humanity, Machines, and the Internet* by Michael Chorost, *The Filter Bubble: What the Internet Is Hiding from You* by Eli Pariser, and *You Are Not a Gadget: A Manifesto* by Jaron Lanier. *The New York Review of Books* 23 June 2011: 33–35. Print.

Online Sources

When you list sources from the Web, you do not need to provide the URL address. However, you must state *Web* as the medium in your entry.

10. Website – citing an entire website

title of website   name of sponsoring organization   date of electronic publication

BBC News. Mobile News Network, 24 May 2011. Web. 6 June 2011.

medium   date of information retrieval

11. Web page – an article from an online newspaper

Often newspapers on the Web do not include page numbers even though the print version did have page numbers. If you cannot find a page number, use "n. pag."

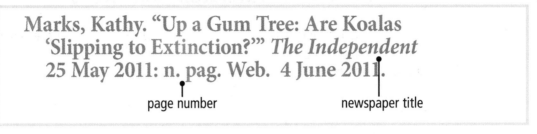

Marks, Kathy. "Up a Gum Tree: Are Koalas 'Slipping to Extinction?'" *The Independent* 25 May 2011: n. pag. Web. 4 June 2011.

page number   newspaper title

Punctuation with Main Clauses

A main clause that stands alone is a sentence and is followed by a period.

William Shakespeare was an Elizabethan playwright.

Two main clauses can be connected to form a compound sentence by using one of the coordinating conjunctions *and, but, yet, so, or,* or *for.* Use a comma (,) before the coordinating conjunction.

William Shakespeare was an important playwright, **but** he also wrote very fine short sonnets.

Two main clauses that are very close in meaning can be connected by a semicolon (;).

Shakespeare's *Romeo and Juliet* is one of his most popular tragedies; it is performed throughout the world.

Punctuation with Transitions

When transitions begin a sentence, they are separated from the main clause by a comma. Common expressions include *for example, moreover, however, therefore, first, next,* and *in fact.*

I enjoy writing in my journal. **However,** I don't like writing letters.

When transitions join two sentences, they are preceded by a semicolon and followed by a comma.

I enjoy writing in my journal; **however,** I don't like writing letters.

Punctuation with Main and Dependent Clauses

Some subordinating conjunctions that introduce dependent clauses include *because, when, before, although,* and *since.*

When the dependent clause begins a sentence, place a comma after it.

When I read my speech at graduation, all my friends and family were amazed.

When the dependent clause comes at the end of the sentence, omit the comma.

All my friends and family were amazed when I read my speech at graduation.

Punctuation with Conditional Sentences

When the *if* clause begins the sentence, use a comma.

If I get a new job**,** I will make more money.

When the *if* clause follows the main clause, do not use a comma.

I will make more money **if** I get the new job.

Punctuation with Relative Clauses

In restrictive clauses use the relative pronouns *who* or *that* for people, *which* or *that* for things and animals, and *whose* to show ownership or belonging. Do not use a comma between the noun and the relative pronoun.

The song **that** won first prize was by a famous Nigerian artist.

The Nigerian artist **who** won the award studied at my music school.

In nonrestrictive relative clauses, use *who* for people and *which* for things. Use commas to separate the clause from the rest of the sentence.

Walker Evans**, who** collaborated with the writer James Agee**,** was a famous 20th-century photographer.

The *Mona Lisa***, which** was painted by Leonardo da Vinci**,** hangs in the Louvre.

Connectors with Noun Phrases

The connectors *because of, due to,* and *as a result of* introduce a noun phrase. When the noun phrase comes at the beginning of a sentence, it is followed by a comma. When it comes at the end of a sentence, no comma is used.

Due to the heavy traffic, we were late for class.

We were late for class **due to** the heavy traffic.

Gerunds

Gerunds follow these verbs and constructions.

Verb + Gerund

acknowledge	delay	finish	mind	regret
admit	deny	go	miss	report
appreciate	discuss	involve	practice	resume
avoid	dislike	keep	recall	suggest
celebrate	enjoy	mean	recommend	understand
consider	feel like	mention		

Verb with Preposition + Gerund

adapt to	argue about	care about	depend on
adjust to	ask about	complain about	disapprove of
agree on	believe in	consist of	forgive for
apologize for	blame for	decide on	help with

Be + Adjective + Preposition + Gerund

be afraid of	be glad about	be known for	be successful in
be angry about	be happy about	be nervous about	be tired of
be concerned with	be interested in	be proud of	be upset about
be familiar with	be jealous of	be sad about	be used for

Infinitives

Infinitives follow these verbs and constructions.

Verb + Infinitive

agree	claim	fail	plan	seem
appear	decide	hope	pretend	struggle
arrange	decline	intend	refuse	volunteer
care	demand	manage	resolve	wait

Verb + Object + Infinitive

advise	get	persuade	tell
command	hire	remind	trust
convince	invite	require	urge
force	order	teach	warn

Verb + (Object) + Infinitive

ask	desire	need	promise
beg	expect	offer	want
choose	help	pay	wish
dare	know	prepare	would like

Adapted from the *Oxford Dictionary of American English*

Glossary of Grammatical Terms

action verb a verb that describes a thing that someone or something does. An action verb does not describe a state or condition.

> Sam **rang** the bell.
> It **rains** a lot here.

active sentence in active sentences, the agent (the noun that is performing the action) is in subject position, and the receiver (the noun that receives or is a result of the action) is in object position. In the following sentence, the subject *Alex* performed the action, and the object *letter* received the action.

> Alex mailed the letter.

adjective a word that describes or modifies the meaning of a noun.

> the **orange** car   a **strange** noise

adverb a word that describes or modifies the meaning of a verb, another adverb, an adjective, or a sentence. Many adverbs answer such questions as *How? When? Where?* or *How often?* They often end in *–ly*.

> She ran **quickly.**   She ran **very** quickly.
> a **really** hot day   **Maybe** she'll leave.

adverbial phrase a phrase that functions as an adverb.

> Ali spoke **very softly.**

affirmative statement a sentence that does not have a negative verb.

> Lin went to the movies.

agreement the subject and verb of a clause must agree in number. If the subject is singular, the verb form is also singular. If the subject is plural, the verb form is also plural.

> **He comes** home early.   **They come** home early.

article the words *a, an,* and *the* in English. Articles are used to introduce and identify nouns.

> **a** mango   **an** onion   **the** market

auxiliary verb a verb that is used before main verbs (or other auxiliary verbs) in a sentence. Auxiliary verbs are usually used in questions and negative sentences. *Do, have,* and *be* can act as auxiliary verbs. Modals (*may, can, will*) are also auxiliary verbs.

> **Do** you have the time?   The car **was** speeding.
> I **have** never been to Mali.   I **may** be late.

base form the form of a verb without any verb endings; the infinitive form without to.

> sleep   be   stop

clause a group of words that has a subject and a verb. *See also* **dependent clause** and **main clause**.

> If I leave, ... when he speaks.
> The rain stopped.   . . . that I saw.

common noun a noun that refers to any of a class of people, animals, places, things, or ideas. Common nouns are not capitalized.

> man   cat   city   pencil   grammar

comparative a form of an adjective, adverb, or noun that is used to express differences between two items or situations.

> This book is **heavier than** that one.
> He runs **more quickly than** his brother.
> The DVD costs **more money than** the CD.

complex sentence a sentence that has a main clause and one or more dependent clauses.

> When the bell rang, we were finishing dinner.

compound sentence a sentence that has two main clauses separated by a comma and a conjunction, or by a semi-colon.

> She is very talented; she can sing and dance.

conditional sentence a sentence that expresses a real or unreal situation in the *if* clause, and the (real or unreal) expected result in the main clause.

> If I have time, I will travel to Africa.
> If I had time, I would travel to Africa.

count noun a common noun that can be counted. It usually has both a singular and a plural form.

> orange — oranges   woman — women

definite article the word *the* in English. It is used to identify nouns based on assumptions about what information the speaker and listener share about the noun. The definite article is also used for making general statements about a whole class or group of nouns.

> Please give me **the** key.
> **The** scorpion is dangerous.

dependent clause a clause that cannot stand alone as a sentence because it depends on the main clause to complete the meaning of the sentence. Also called *subordinate clause.*

> I'm going home **after he calls.**

determiner a word such *as a, an, the, this, that, these, those, my, some, a few,* and any number that is used before a noun to limit its meaning in some way.

> **those** videos

future a time that is to come. The future is expressed in English with *will, be going to,* the simple present, or the present continuous. These different forms of the future often have different meanings and uses.

> I **will** help you later.
> David **is going to** call later.
> The train **leaves** at 6:05 this evening.
> I**'m driving** to Toronto tomorrow.

gerund an *-ing* form of a verb that is used in place of a noun or pronoun to name an activity or a state.

> **Skiing** is fun.   He doesn't like **being sick**.

if **clause** a dependent clause that begins with *if* and expresses a real or unreal situation.

> **If I have the time,** I'll paint the kitchen.
> **If I had the time,** I'd paint the kitchen.

indefinite article the words *a* and *an* in English. Indefinite articles introduce a noun as a member of a class of nouns or make generalizations about a whole class or group of nouns.

> **An** ocean is **a** large body of water.

independent clause *See* **main clause.**

indirect object a noun or pronoun used after some verbs that refers to the person who receives the direct object of a sentence.

> Fatima wrote a letter to **Mary.**
> Please buy some milk for **us.**

infinitive a verb form that includes *to* + the base form of a verb. An infinitive is used in place of a noun or pronoun to name an activity or situation expressed by a verb.

> Do you like **to swim?**

intransitive verb a verb that cannot be followed by an object.

> We finally **arrived.**

main clause a clause that can be used by itself as a sentence. Also called *independent clause.*

> I'm going home.

main verb a verb that can be used alone in a sentence. A main verb can also occur with an auxiliary verb.

> I **ate** lunch at 11:30.
> Tsutomu can't **eat** lunch today.

modal the auxiliary verbs *can, could, may, might, must, should, will,* and *would.* They modify the meaning of a main verb by expressing ability, authority, formality,

politeness, or various degrees of certainty. Also called *modal auxiliary.*

> You **should** take something for your headache.
> Applicants **must** have a high school diploma.

negative statement a sentence with a negative verb.

> I **didn't see** that movie.

noun a word that typically refers to a person, animal, place, thing, or idea.

> Tom   rabbit   store   computer   mathematics

noun clause a dependent clause that can occur in the same place as a noun, pronoun, or noun phrase in a sentence. Noun clauses begin with *wh-* words, *if, whether,* or *that.*

> I don't know **where he is.**
> I wonder **if he's coming.**
> I don't know **whether it's true.**
> I think **that it's a lie.**

noun phrase a phrase formed by a noun and its modifiers. A noun phrase can substitute for a noun in a sentence.

> She drank **juice.**
> She drank **orange juice.**
> She drank **the orange juice.**

object a noun, pronoun, or noun phrase that follows a transitive verb or a preposition.

> He likes **sushi.**   Go with **her.**
> She likes **him.**   Sanjay threw **the ball.**

passive sentence passive sentences emphasize the receiver of an action by changing the usual order of the subject and object in a sentence. In the sentence below, the subject *(The letter)* does not perform the action; it receives the action or is the result of an action. The passive is formed with a form of *be* + the past participle of a transitive verb.

> The letter was mailed yesterday.

past continuous a verb form that expresses an action or situation in progress at a specific time in the past. The past continuous is formed with *was* or *were* + verb + *-ing.* Also called **past progressive.**

> A: What **were** you **doing** last night at eight o'clock?
> B: I **was studying.**

past participle A past verb form that may differ from the simple past form of some irregular verbs. It is used to form the present perfect.

> I have never **seen** that movie.

phrasal verb a two- or three-word verb such as *turn down* or *run out of.* The meaning of a phrasal verb is usually different from the meanings of its individual words.

> She **turned down** the job offer.
> Don't **run out of** gas on the freeway.

phrase a group of words that can form a grammatical unit. A phrase can take the form of a noun phrase, verb phrase, adjective phrase, adverbial phrase, or prepositional phrase. This means it can act as a noun, verb, adjective, adverb, or preposition.

The **tall man** left.   She spoke **too fast**.
Lee **hit the ball**.   They ran **down the stairs**.

preposition a word such as *at, in, on,* or *to,* that links nouns, pronouns, and gerunds to other words.

prepositional phrase a phrase that consists of a preposition followed by a noun or noun phrase.

on Monday   under the table

present continuous a verb form that indicates that an activity is in progress, temporary, or changing. It is formed with *be* + verb + *–ing*. Also called *present progressive*.

I **am watering** the garden.
Ramya **is working** for her uncle.

present perfect a verb form that expresses a connection between the past and the present. It indicates indefinite past time, recent past time, or continuing past time. The present perfect is formed with *have* + the past participle of the main verb.

I **have seen** that movie.
The manager **has** just **resigned**.
We**'ve been** here for three hours.

pronoun a word that can replace a noun or noun phrase. *I, you, he, she, it, mine,* and *yours* are some examples of pronouns.

quantity expression a word or words that occur before a noun to express a quantity or amount of that noun.

a lot of rain   **few** books   **four** trucks

simple past a verb form that expresses actions and situations that were completed at a definite time in the past.

Carol **ate** lunch.   She **was** hungry.

simple present a verb form that expresses general statements, especially about habitual or repeated activities and permanent situations.

Every morning I **catch** the 8:00 bus.
The earth **is** round.

stative verb a type of verb that is not usually used in the continuous form because it expresses a condition or state that is not changing. *Know, love, see,* and *smell* are some examples.

subject a noun, pronoun, or noun phrase that precedes the verb phrase in a sentence. The subject is closely related to the verb as the doer or experiencer of the action or state, or closely related to the noun that is being described in a sentence with *be*.

Erica kicked the ball.
The park is huge.

subordinate clause *See* **dependent clause**.

superlative a form of an adjective, adverb, or noun that is used to rank an item or situation first or last in a group of three or more.

This perfume has **the strongest** scent.
He speaks **the fastest** of all.
That machine makes **the most noise** of the three.

tense the form of a verb that shows past, present, and future time.

He **lives** in Dalian now.
He **lived** in Shanghai two years ago.
He**'ll live** in Suzhou next year.

time clause a dependent clause that begins with a word such as *while, when, before,* or *after*. It expresses the relationship in time between two different events in the same sentence.

Before Sandra left, she fixed the copy machine.

time expression a phrase that functions as an adverb of time.

She graduated **three years ago**.
I'll see them the **day after tomorrow**.

transitive verb a verb that is followed by an object.

I **read** the book.

uncountable (noncount) noun a common noun that cannot be counted. A noncount noun has no plural form and cannot occur with *a, an,* or a number.

information   mathematics   weather

verb a word that refers to an action or a state.

Alexandr **closed** the window.
Yasuko **loves** classical music.

verb phrase a phrase that has a main verb and any objects, adverbs, or dependent clauses that complete the meaning of the verb in the sentence.

Who **called you**?
He **walked slowly**.

Glossary of Research Terms

academic journal a periodical that is reviewed by scholars from the same academic discipline.

annotated notes added to a text to explain and give extra information about the content.

anonymous a name that is not known or made public.

archives a collection of historical documents, etc., that record the history of a place or an organization; the place where they are kept.

artifacts an object that is made by a person, especially something of historical or cultural interest.

citation a reference in a speech or piece of writing to something that somebody else has said or written.

cite to mention something as an example to support what you are saying.

copyright the legal rights to a piece of original work, such as a book, a song, or a computer program.

credible source trustworthy information that comes from reputable books, people, etc.

database a large amount of data that is stored in a computer and can easily be used, added to, or revised.

EBSCO database full text database used for academic research.

keyword 1 a word that you type into a computer to search for information about a particular subject; 2 a word that tells you about the main idea or subject of something.

narrow a topic down to make a topic more manageable by focusing on a specific aspect or subtopic.

paraphrase 1 to express the meaning of something using different words; 2 a rewording of a passage.

parenthetical citation a tool used within the text of a book, paper, etc., that identifies where the information originated and refers to the Works Cited list.

plagiarism taking someone else's ideas or words and using them as if they were your own.

primary source original materials such as legal documents, artifacts, letters, interviews, or speeches.

quote 1 to repeat exactly something someone has said or written before; 2 to give someone else's words as an example to support your ideas.

reference a note that tells you where certain information can be found.

reliable source trustworthy information that comes from reputable books, people, etc.

relevant/relevance connected to what is being discussed or happening.

search engine a computer program that searches the Internet for information, especially by looking for documents containing a particular word or group of words.

secondary source a source that has been analyzed and/or explained by a third party. Secondary sources include books, magazines, and academic journals.

summarize to write a short description of the main ideas or events of something.

Works Cited a list of sources cited in a researched essay or report. These are arranged in alphabetical order.

Glossary of Academic Terms

acknowledge to accept or admit that something is true or exists.

analyze to look at or think about the different parts or details of something carefully in order to understand or explain it.

anecdote a short, interesting story about a real person or event.

aspect one of the qualities or parts of a situation, idea, problem, etc.

assert to say something clearly and firmly.

assess 1 to judge or form an opinion about something; 2 to estimate or decide the amount or value of something.

categorize to divide people or things into groups; to say that somebody or something belongs to a particular group.

coherent connected in a way that makes sense; clear and easy to understand.

collocation a word or group of words that very often occur together.

compile to collect information and arrange it in a list, book, etc.

concept an idea, a basic principle.

concession a type of counter-argument in which the writer agrees that the opposing point of view is valid but emphasizes how his or her argument is stronger.

conduct to carry out or organize something.

convince to succeed in making somebody believe something; to persuade somebody to do something.

correlate to show a connection or relationship between things.

counter-argument the writer's opinion about the opposing point of view, which gives reasons why the writer's point of view makes sense. By including the counter-argument, the writer shows an understanding of the opposing point of view.

critique to describe the good and bad points of somebody or something.

defend to say or write something to support somebody or something, such as an argument.

distinguish to recognize the difference between things or people.

editorial an article in a newspaper that gives an opinion on an important subject.

estimate a guess or judgment about the size, cost, etc., of something before you have all the facts and figures.

ethical moral.

evidence information indicating whether something is true or valid.

formulate to express something clearly and exactly.

graphic organizer a picture or diagram that is used to arrange information and ideas.

grounds for factors forming a good reason for doing or thinking something.

hypothesis an idea that is suggested as the possible explanation for something.

hypothetical based on situations that have not yet happened, and not on facts.

impact on a strong effect or influence on somebody or something.

infer to reach a conclusion from the information you have.

insightful the ability to understand the truth about someone or something.

interpret to explain or understand the meaning of something.

oppose to disagree with somebody's beliefs, actions, or plans and to try to change or stop them.

outcome how an event, an action, or a situation ends.

point of view a way of looking at a situation or an opinion.

rank to organize in an order of importance.

refutation the writer's response to a counter-argument. In a refutation, the writer shows why a counter-argument is weak and his or her position is strong.

refute to prove that something is wrong.

restrict to limit the number, amount, size, freedom, etc., of somebody or something.

rhetorical mode a method of presenting information in writing. Some common rhetorical modes are argumentative, cause and effect, and classification.

rhetorical question a question that is not really a question because it does not expect an answer.

survey 1 to ask people questions about their habits, opinion, etc., for a study of something; 2 to look at the whole of something; to examine or study something as a whole.

thesaurus a book that contains lists of words and phrases with similar meanings.

EFFECTIVE ACADEMIC WRITING 3: THE RESEARCHED ESSAY	GRAMMAR SENSE 3
UNIT 1 Dependent Clauses	**CHAPTER 2** The Past
UNIT 2 Relative Clauses	**CHAPTER 13** Relative Clauses with Subject Relative Pronouns **CHAPTER 14** Relative Clauses with Object Relative Pronouns
UNIT 3 Conditional Sentences	**CHAPTER 15** Real Conditionals, Unreal Conditionals, and Wishes
UNIT 4 Adverbial Clauses Noun Clauses	**CHAPTER 17** Noun Clauses
UNIT 5 Gerunds and Infinitives	**CHAPTER 11** Contrasting Gerunds and Infinitives
UNIT 6 Passives	**CHAPTER 9** Passive Sentences (Part 1) **CHAPTER 10** Passive Sentences (Part 2)